Ben Halsall.

Salads and Snacks

Salads and Snacks

Carol Bowen

Sundial

Contents

First published in 1978 by Sundial Books Limited
59 Grosvenor Street, London W1

© 1978 Hennerwood Publications Limited

ISBN 0 904230 61 9

Printed in England by Severn Valley Press Limited

Introduction

Salads

There are many delightful surprises in store here for all those who thought that salads could only be served on a hot summer day, and for those, too, who imagine a salad to be the usual greenery served time and time again.

Salads have no special season – simple, easy to prepare green salads with a vinaigrette dressing or mixed vegetable salads make wonderful accompaniments to cold meats, savoury bakes, omelettes and quiches at any time of the year. Salads can also be elaborate enough to become part of a celebration buffet.

The secret to success is simple: always choose fresh, unblemished salad produce and prepare in an imaginative way. Combine flavours and textures of salad ingredients, main meal accompaniments and salad dressings.

* The first step with any salad ingredient is to wash it well. Remove any bruised or damaged parts, such as the outer leaves of cabbages, lettuces, chicory, etc. Trim off unwanted parts, such as the tops and tails of courgettes, spring onions, French beans, etc. And wash again. Pat dry with absorbent kitchen paper or a clean tea towel, or, as with lettuce, shake in a wire mesh basket. (If lettuce is wet, it will dilute the dressing.)

* Always skin *tomatoes* for a salad. Prick the skin with a knife tip, then plunge the tomatoes into a bowl of boiling water. Leave for 1 minute – the skin will begin to curl up where broken. Lift out with a perforated spoon and plunge immediately into cold water so that the tomatoes remain firm. The skin will then peel off easily.

* Use raw *carrots* grated – they are much more digestible this way. For decorative curls, pare large carrots with a vegetable peeler and shave off strips lengthways. Roll the curls around the fingertip and chill in iced water. Use as a decorative garnish.

* The peel on *cucumber* is attractive so don't always cut it away. Draw the prongs of a fork firmly down the surface lengthways, repeat all round and then slice for attractive fluted circles.

* Plunge *eggs* immediately into cold water the minute they are boiled to prevent further cooking and dark unattractive rings around the yolks. Peel and resubmerge in cold water to keep the whites moist.

* If you want just a hint of *garlic*, cut a clove of garlic in two, then rub the cut edge around the inside of the salad bowl before tossing the salad. Or leave the garlic clove in the salad oil for a time before preparing the dressing.

* *Spring onions* have a delicate flavour that blends well with lettuce. Wash and trim off the roots and 5 cm (2 inches) off the tops before chopping the white and green parts of the stalks. Chopped raw *leek* can be mixed in a salad at other times of the year.

* Cut *fruit* such as apples, bananas or avocados at the very last moment and dip in lemon juice to prevent them from turning brown. When orange or grapefruit segments are used, peel the fruit with a serrated-edge knife to remove all the white pith.

* Wash *lettuce* clean by dunking it head first, up and down, in a bowl of cold water – the suction action draws out the dirt. Separate the leaves but take care not to bruise them. Fold lightly in a clean tea towel and swing it until the leaves are dry; alternatively use a wire salad basket for this.

* *Herbs* enhance the flavours of a salad. Use chervil, mint, parsley and chives generously. Wash and pat dry with absorbent kitchen paper. Hold a bunch over your salad bowl and snip with kitchen scissors.

* Whole or chopped *nuts* can provide an interesting texture, but do not add until the last minute to preserve the crunchiness.

* Malt vinegar is too harsh for salad *dressings*; wine, cider or herb-flavoured vinegars provide more subtle flavours. Lemon juice can be used in place of some or all of the vinegar if you prefer. Mix salad dressings in a screw-topped jar by shaking vigorously. Any dressing not used can then easily be stored in the refrigerator. Pour dressings over salads shortly before serving or the lettuce will become limp.

When salads are to provide a main meal they should contain some vital protein food such as egg, meat, chicken, cheese or fish.

* *Eggs* which have been hard-boiled can be stuffed with savoury mixtures. Remove the yolks from the egg halves and mash with a spoonful of mayonnaise and ingredients such as canned sardines, pounded anchovies, smoked buckling pâté or grated cheese. Pile the mixture back into the egg white shells.

* Delicatessen *cooked meats* and continental slicing sausages are delicious eaten cold. Fold on a platter with other cold meats or twist into cones that look attractive set around the edge of a platter. Use to wrap chunks of cheese or fruit.

   Remember, too, that it is often more economical to serve a cooked roast of meat cold. Let a roast stand overnight and it will retain most of its juiciness, then slice it very thinly. If you brush a little liquid aspic or consommé over the slices and chill until set, they will have a shiny and tasty finish.

* *Cheese* chosen carefully can provide plenty of protein without too many calories. Cottage cheese, the obvious favourite with weight-watchers, can be mixed with a number of ingredients: chopped cooked prunes, freshly chopped herbs, seedless raisins, chopped apple or grated carrot.

   Hard cheeses are more adaptable when grated for salads, while some of the closer-textured cheeses, such as Edam, are better cut into fingers or cubes.

* *Fish* makes a tasty salad ingredient. Frozen shrimps, prawns and cooked scallops are delicious when mixed with mayonnaise and lemon juice and piled onto lettuce.

   Smoked fish fillets are ideal for occasions when you really need to pull something special out of the hat. Try smoked salmon slices rolled around asparagus tips, or fillets of smoked mackerel with lemon quarters and hard-boiled egg.

* Choose crusty *breads* to serve with salad meals – newly baked cottage and farmhouse loaves and French sticks which can be broken or cut into chunks for serving. Wheatmeal or wholemeal bread with cracked wheat on top looks especially appetizing. Soft baps or crisp rolls, particularly those with poppy or sesame seeds baked on the outside, look and taste good too.

   Explore the flavours of continental rye, caraway seed and pumpernickel as well as the less known German Landbrot. Rye bread goes well with both continental slicing sausages and cheese, while pumpernickel is very good with smoked ham.

All dishes serve 4 unless otherwise stated.

Snacks

One eye on the clock and a hurried sandwich is many people's idea of a snack. But with a little forethought and the use of ready-prepared products, you can produce some enjoyable mini-meals.

Organization is the key word. Never be caught without those versatile store-cupboard ingredients such as canned fish, soups, cooked meats, rice and pasta, and frozen pastry.

Don't forget, either, to keep a plentiful supply of cheese and eggs, which form the basis of many snacks. Liven up an omelette with a new filling or a jacket potato with a golden topping.

Add a crispy salad to your snack meal and you have the makings of an expansible feast.

SIDE SALADS

Tossed green salad

Metric

½ lettuce, separated into leaves
¼ bunch of curly endive
½ bunch of watercress
¼ cucumber, sliced
1 green pepper, cored, seeded and sliced
Few spring onions
120 ml French dressing

Imperial

½ lettuce, separated into leaves
¼ bunch of curly endive
½ bunch of watercress
¼ cucumber, sliced
1 green pepper, cored, seeded and sliced
Few spring onions
4 fl oz French dressing

Put all the vegetables in a deep salad bowl. Pour over the dressing and toss well.

A basic green salad can be varied in many ways. Try adding any of the following:
Apple wedges: Use red eating apples, cored and thinly sliced.
Avocado slivers: Halve avocados, remove the stones, peel and slice the flesh. Toss in lemon juice to prevent them turning brown.
Cauliflower sprigs: Break the cauliflower into small sprigs and use raw.
Cheese: Use any kind, grated, sliced or cubed.
Egg: Hard-boil and thinly slice before adding.
Fresh herbs: Wash, dry and add, either chopped or in sprigs.
Grapefruit or oranges: Cut away the peel and white pith and break the fruit into segments.
Olives: Drain from jar and use whole or sliced.
Nuts: Use whole or coarsely chopped; add at the very last minute.

Winter salad

Metric

4 medium waxy potatoes, peeled, cooked and diced
1 large celery stalk, finely chopped
2 carrots, peeled and grated
1 small onion, peeled and finely chopped
½ small white cabbage, cored and shredded
2 × 15 ml spoons chopped pickled gherkins
8 black olives, stoned and chopped
120 ml French dressing
2 × 15 ml spoons finely chopped fresh parsley

Imperial

4 medium waxy potatoes, peeled, cooked and diced
1 large celery stalk, finely chopped
2 carrots, peeled and grated
1 small onion, peeled and finely chopped
½ small white cabbage, cored and shredded
2 tablespoons chopped pickled gherkins
8 black olives, stoned and chopped
4 fl oz French dressing
2 tablespoons finely chopped fresh parsley

Put the potatoes, celery, carrots, onion, cabbage, gherkins and olives in a salad bowl. Pour over the French dressing and toss well. Sprinkle with the chopped fresh parsley and serve.
Serves 6

Courgette and chive salad

Metric	Imperial
350 g courgettes	12 oz courgettes
1 × 15 ml spoon olive oil	1 tablespoon olive oil
2 × 15 ml spoons lemon juice	2 tablespoons lemon juice
Large pinch of salt	Large pinch of salt
Large pinch of freshly ground black pepper	Large pinch of freshly ground black pepper
1 × 15 ml spoon chopped fresh chives	1 tablespoon chopped fresh chives

Bring a large pan of lightly salted water to the boil. Drop in the courgettes and cook for 5 minutes. Drain and rinse in cold water.

Cut the courgettes crossways into 1 cm (½ inch) slices and place in a shallow serving dish.

Mix together the oil, lemon juice, salt and pepper and pour over the courgettes. Sprinkle with the chopped chives and chill for about 30 minutes before serving.

Waldorf salad

Metric	Imperial
500 g tart red eating apples, cored	1 lb tart red eating apples, cored
2 × 15 ml spoons lemon juice	2 tablespoons lemon juice
1 × 5 ml spoon caster sugar	1 teaspoon caster sugar
150 ml mayonnaise	¼ pint mayonnaise
½ head of celery, chopped	½ head of celery, chopped
50 g shelled walnuts, chopped	2 oz shelled walnuts, chopped
1 lettuce, separated into leaves	1 lettuce, separated into leaves

Slice one apple thinly and dice the remainder. Dip the apple slices in a dressing made with the lemon juice, caster sugar and 1 × 15 ml spoon (1 tablespoon) of the mayonnaise. Set aside. Toss the diced apple in the remaining dressing and let it stand for 30 minutes.

Add the celery and walnuts to the diced apple with the rest of the mayonnaise and mix thoroughly. Line a serving bowl with the lettuce leaves, pile the salad in the centre and garnish with the apple slices.

Courgette and chive salad; Chicory and orange salad

Salad elona

Metric

1 small cucumber, peeled
and thinly sliced
12 large strawberries,
hulled and thinly sliced
Large pinch of salt
Large pinch of freshly
ground black pepper
2 × 15 ml spoons dry
white wine

Imperial

1 small cucumber, peeled
and thinly sliced
12 large strawberries,
hulled and thinly sliced
Large pinch of salt
Large pinch of freshly
ground black pepper
2 tablespoons dry
white wine

Arrange the cucumber and strawberry slices decoratively on a shallow serving dish – an outer circle of cucumber, slightly overlapped by a circle of strawberry slices, then more cucumber, finishing with a centre of strawberry slices. Sprinkle over the salt, pepper and wine and chill for about 20 minutes before serving.

Chicory and orange salad

Metric

4 heads of chicory, cut
crossways into 5 mm
thick slices
3 oranges, peeled, white
pith removed, and thinly
sliced across the segments
6 × 15 ml spoons olive oil
2 × 15 ml spoons orange
juice
Large pinch of salt
Large pinch of freshly
ground black pepper

Imperial

4 heads of chicory, cut
crossways into ¼ inch
thick slices
3 oranges, peeled, white
pith removed, and thinly
sliced across the segments
6 tablespoons olive oil
2 tablespoons orange
juice
Large pinch of salt
Large pinch of freshly
ground black pepper

Put the chicory and orange slices in a serving bowl. Shake together the olive oil, orange juice, salt and pepper in a screw-topped jar. Pour this dressing over the chicory and orange slices. Toss and serve at once.

Salad elona; Waldorf salad

Leeks à la niçoise

Metric	Imperial
1 kg young leeks	2 lb young leeks
4 × 15 ml spoons olive oil	4 tablespoons olive oil
Salt	Salt
Freshly ground black pepper	Freshly ground black pepper
225 g tomatoes, skinned and chopped	8 oz tomatoes, skinned and chopped
1 small garlic clove, crushed	1 small garlic clove, crushed
1 × 15 ml spoon finely chopped fresh parsley	1 tablespoon finely chopped fresh parsley
Lemon juice	Lemon juice

Cooking time: 20 minutes

Cut the leeks, so they are an even length. Heat the oil in a flameproof casserole. Put in the leeks, side by side. Fry until lightly coloured underneath, turn and season lightly with salt and pepper. Cover the casserole and cook the leeks gently for 10 minutes. Lift out the leeks and keep warm.

Add the tomatoes to the pan with the garlic and parsley and cook briskly for 3 to 5 minutes, stirring constantly. Adjust seasoning and sharpen with lemon juice. Return the leeks to the sauce and serve hot, or chill and serve cold.

French beans mimosa

Metric	Imperial
500 g young French beans	1 lb young French beans
6 × 15 ml spoons olive oil	6 tablespoons olive oil
2 × 15 ml spoons lemon juice	2 tablespoons lemon juice
1 hard-boiled egg to garnish	1 hard-boiled egg to garnish

Cook the beans in boiling, salted water for 6 to 8 minutes. Drain and arrange on a round shallow serving dish, radiating from the centre.

Mix together the olive oil and the lemon juice and pour over the warm beans. Leave to cool.

Separate the white and yolk of the egg. Chop the white finely and rub the yolk through a coarse sieve.

Before serving, garnish the beans by arranging the egg white in the centre of the dish and scattering the egg yolk along the beans to resemble mimosa.

Napoleon's bean salad

Metric

225 g dried haricot beans
1 onion, peeled and
quartered
1 carrot, peeled and
quartered
1 bouquet garni
Freshly ground black
pepper
Salt
4 × 15 ml spoons finely
chopped fresh herbs
(parsley, tarragon, chives
or spring onions)
5 × 15 ml spoons olive oil
1 × 15 ml spoon tarragon
vinegar
1 × 5 ml spoon prepared
French mustard
1 × 2.5 ml spoon caster
sugar

Imperial

8 oz dried haricot beans
1 onion, peeled and
quartered
1 carrot, peeled and
quartered
1 bouquet garni
Freshly ground black
pepper
Salt
4 tablespoons finely
chopped fresh herbs
(parsley, tarragon, chives
or spring onions)
5 tablespoons olive oil
1 tablespoon tarragon
vinegar
1 teaspoon prepared
French mustard
½ teaspoon caster
sugar

Cooking time: 3 hours
Oven: 150°C, 300°F, Gas Mark 2

Soak the beans in water for 8 hours or overnight. Drain the beans and put them in a large pan or casserole. Add the onion and carrot quarters, bouquet garni and plenty of black pepper. Pour over sufficient water to cover the beans by 1 cm (½ inch). Cook in the centre of a preheated cool oven for 3 hours, or on top of the stove for 2 to 3 hours at simmering point. Replace any water so that the beans do not dry out.

Season the cooked beans to taste with salt and cook for a further 5 minutes. Drain, then remove and discard the onion, carrot and bouquet garni. Place the beans in a large serving bowl. Add the chopped herbs, oil, vinegar, mustard and sugar. Stir to mix. Chill for about 1 hour before serving.
Serves 6

Napoleon's bean salad

Bean sprout salad

Metric	Imperial
225 g fresh or canned bean sprouts, drained	*8 oz fresh or canned bean sprouts, drained*
1 canned pimiento, drained and chopped	*1 canned pimiento, drained and chopped*
1 pickled cucumber, diced	*1 pickled cucumber, diced*
1 × 15 ml spoon finely chopped fresh chives	*1 tablespoon finely chopped fresh chives*

Dressing:
2 × 15 ml spoons olive oil	*2 tablespoons olive oil*
1 × 15 ml spoon wine vinegar	*1 tablespoon wine vinegar*
1 × 2.5 ml spoon prepared mustard	*½ teaspoon prepared mustard*
2 × 5 ml spoons soy sauce	*2 teaspoons soy sauce*
1 × 2.5 ml spoon sugar	*½ teaspoon sugar*
1 × 2.5 ml spoon salt	*½ teaspoon salt*

Put the bean sprouts in a salad bowl with the pimiento, pickled cucumber and chives.

Mix together all the ingredients for the dressing making sure that the sugar and salt are completely dissolved. Pour the dressing over the salad and toss to coat thoroughly. Chill for about 30 minutes before serving.

Bean sprout salad

Sweet and sour salad

Metric

4 medium eating apples,
peeled, cored and diced
1 medium grapefruit,
peeled, white pith removed
and finely chopped
1 pickled cucumber, thinly
sliced
75 g fresh or canned
pineapple, chopped
2 heads of chicory, thinly
sliced
1 × 15 ml spoon finely
chopped fresh coriander

Dressing:
1 × 15 ml spoon clear
honey
1 × 15 ml spoon lemon
juice
1 × 15 ml spoon grated
lemon rind
2 × 15 ml spoons oil
1 × 15 ml spoon cider
vinegar
1 × 5 ml spoon salt
1 × 2.5 ml spoon white
pepper

Imperial

4 medium eating apples,
peeled, cored and diced
1 medium grapefruit,
peeled, white pith removed
and finely chopped
1 pickled cucumber, thinly
sliced
3 oz fresh or canned
pineapple, chopped
2 heads of chicory, thinly
sliced
1 tablespoon finely
chopped fresh coriander

Dressing:
1 tablespoon clear
honey
1 tablespoon lemon
juice
1 tablespoon grated
lemon rind
2 tablespoons oil
1 tablespoon cider
vinegar
1 teaspoon salt
½ teaspoon white
pepper

Put the apples, grapefruit, cucumber, pineapple and chicory in a large salad bowl and mix well.

Shake together the dressing ingredients in a screw-topped jar. Pour the dressing over the salad and toss well. Cover and place in the refrigerator. Chill for 1 hour.

Just before serving stir in the coriander.

Gruyère and mushroom salad

Metric

225 g Gruyère cheese, cut
into small cubes
100 g button mushrooms,
quartered
4 large lettuce leaves
1 × 15 ml spoon finely
chopped fresh parsley

Dressing:
6 × 15 ml spoons olive oil
2 × 15 ml spoons red wine
vinegar
1 garlic clove, crushed
1 × 2.5 ml spoon salt
Large pinch of freshly
ground black pepper

Imperial

8 oz Gruyère cheese, cut
into small cubes
4 oz button mushrooms,
quartered
4 large lettuce leaves
1 tablespoon finely
chopped fresh parsley

Dressing:
6 tablespoons olive oil
2 tablespoons red wine
vinegar
1 garlic clove, crushed
½ teaspoon salt
Large pinch of freshly
ground black pepper

Put all the dressing ingredients in a screw-topped jar and shake until well mixed. Place the cheese and mushrooms in a mixing bowl and pour over the dressing. Toss to coat and leave for 20 minutes.

Line a shallow salad bowl with the lettuce leaves. Spoon the cheese mixture on top of the lettuce and sprinkle with the chopped parsley. Serve at once.

Sweet and sour salad (behind); Gruyère and mushroom salad

Clockwise: Beetroot and egg salad (top left); Fennel salad;
Mushroom salad; Celery, apple and walnut salad; Tomato salad

Beetroot and egg salad

Metric

*500 g beetroots, cooked,
peeled and cooled
1 medium onion, peeled
and sliced into rings
4 hard-boiled eggs
120 ml French dressing
2 × 15 ml spoons finely
chopped fresh parsley*

Imperial

*1 lb beetroots, cooked,
peeled and cooled
1 medium onion, peeled
and sliced into rings
4 hard-boiled eggs
4 fl oz French dressing
2 tablespoons finely
chopped fresh parsley*

Grate the beetroots into a serving bowl. Stir in the onion.
Slice the eggs in half and remove the yolks. Rub the yolks
through a strainer into the bowl. Set the whites aside.
Pour the dressing over the beetroot mixture and toss gently
together. Finely chop the egg whites and sprinkle them
over the salad with the parsley. Serve immediately.

Fennel salad

Metric

3 medium heads of fennel, chopped
1 small eating apple, peeled, cored and sliced
2 medium tomatoes, skinned and diced
2 spring onions, diced
120 ml French dressing

Imperial

3 medium heads of fennel, chopped
1 small eating apple, peeled, cored and sliced
2 medium tomatoes, skinned and diced
2 spring onions, diced
4 fl oz French dressing

Put the fennel in a salad bowl. Add the apple, tomatoes and spring onions and stir to mix.
Pour over the French dressing and toss well. Chill in the refrigerator for 1 hour before serving, stirring occasionally.

Tomato salad

Metric

12 tomatoes, skinned and thinly sliced
4 × 15 ml spoons olive oil
4 × 5 ml spoons white wine vinegar
2 × 5 ml spoons caster sugar
Salt
Freshly ground black pepper
1 × 15 ml spoon finely chopped fresh chives or tarragon

Imperial

12 tomatoes, skinned and thinly sliced
4 tablespoons olive oil
4 teaspoons white wine vinegar
2 teaspoons caster sugar
Salt
Freshly ground black pepper
1 tablespoon finely chopped fresh chives or tarragon

Place the tomatoes in a shallow salad dish. Mix together the oil, vinegar, sugar and salt and pepper to taste. Pour over the tomatoes. Sprinkle with the chives or tarragon. Chill for at least 1 hour before serving.
Serves 6

Mushroom salad

Metric

500 g button mushrooms, thinly sliced
Large pinch of salt
Large pinch of freshly ground black pepper
2 × 5 ml spoons Worcestershire sauce
1 × 15 ml spoon soy sauce

Imperial

1 lb button mushrooms, thinly sliced
Large pinch of salt
Large pinch of freshly ground black pepper
2 teaspoons Worcestershire sauce
1 tablespoon soy sauce

Put the mushrooms in a deep serving dish. Sprinkle with the salt, pepper and Worcestershire and soy sauces. Toss to coat thoroughly. Leave for 1 hour.
By the time the mushrooms are to be served, quite a lot of juice will have drained from them. This is an essential part of the salad dressing and should not be drained off.

Celery, apple and walnut salad

Metric

1 medium head of celery, finely chopped
4 red eating apples, cored and diced
2 × 15 spoons French dressing
3 × 15 ml spoons mayonnaise
50 g shelled walnuts, chopped

Imperial

1 medium head of celery, finely chopped
4 red eating apples, cored and diced
2 tablespoons French dressing
3 tablespoons mayonnaise
2 oz shelled walnuts, chopped

Mix together the celery, apples, French dressing and mayonnaise in a salad bowl. Chill for 30 minutes.
Just before serving, stir in the walnuts.

Apple and celeriac salad

Metric

750 g celeriac
1 × 5 ml spoon salt
5 × 15 ml spoons
mayonnaise
1 × 15 ml spoon finely
chopped fresh chervil or
borage
1 × 15 ml spoon finely
chopped fresh parsley
2 crisp red eating apples,
cored and thinly sliced
into rings
100 g salted cashew nuts,
finely chopped

Imperial

1½ lb celeriac
1 teaspoon salt
5 tablespoons
mayonnaise
1 tablespoon finely
chopped fresh chervil or
borage
1 tablespoon finely
chopped fresh parsley
2 crisp red eating apples,
cored and thinly sliced
into rings
4 oz salted cashew nuts,
finely chopped

Put the celeriac in a saucepan and cover with water. Add the salt. Bring to the boil, reduce the heat and cook for 15 minutes. Drain thoroughly, allow to cool, then slice thinly. Mix together the mayonnaise, chervil or borage and parsley. Add the apple and celeriac slices and stir to coat. Transfer to a salad bowl. Sprinkle the nuts over the top and serve.
Serves 6

Yorkshire ploughboy

Metric

1 small red cabbage, cored
and very finely shredded
1 onion, peeled and thinly
sliced
1 × 15 ml spoon dark
treacle
2 × 15 ml spoons white
wine vinegar
1 × 2.5 ml spoon prepared
mustard
1 × 2.5 ml spoon salt
1 × 2.5 ml spoon freshly
ground black pepper

Imperial

1 small red cabbage, cored
and very finely shredded
1 onion, peeled and thinly
sliced
1 tablespoon dark
treacle
2 tablespoons white
wine vinegar
½ teaspoon prepared
mustard
½ teaspoon salt
½ teaspoon freshly
ground black pepper

Place the cabbage and onion in a large serving dish. Mix well.
Mix together the treacle, vinegar, mustard, salt and pepper. Pour the dressing over the cabbage mixture and toss together. Serve at once.

Caesar salad

Metric

120 ml French dressing
1 garlic clove
2 × 15 ml spoons oil
3 slices of bread, cut into
small dice
2 crisp lettuces,
separated into leaves
50 g Parmesan cheese,
grated

Imperial

4 fl oz French dressing
1 garlic clove
2 tablespoons oil
3 slices of bread, cut into
small dice
2 crisp lettuces,
separated into leaves
2 oz Parmesan cheese,
grated

In a screw-topped jar, combine the French dressing and garlic. Leave for 1 hour.
Heat the oil in a frying pan. Add the diced bread and fry for 3 to 4 minutes, turning constantly, or until the croûtons are crisp and lightly browned. Remove from the heat. Drain the croûtons on absorbent kitchen paper and allow to cool. Tear the lettuce leaves into small pieces and place in a salad bowl. Remove and discard the garlic from the dressing and pour the dressing over the lettuce leaves. Toss to coat well. Sprinkle over the cheese and top with the croûtons. Serve at once.

Apple and celeriac salad (top); Yorkshire ploughboy; Caesar salad

Coleslaw with Italian dressing

Metric	Imperial
1 medium white cabbage, cored and finely shredded	*1 medium white cabbage, cored and finely shredded*
4 medium carrots, peeled and grated	*4 medium carrots, peeled and grated*
1 small garlic clove, crushed	*1 small garlic clove, crushed*
6 × 15 ml spoons olive oil	*6 tablespoons olive oil*
2 × 15 ml spoons white wine vinegar	*2 tablespoons white wine vinegar*
Large pinch of dried oregano	*Large pinch of dried oregano*
Large pinch of crushed fennel seeds	*Large pinch of crushed fennel seeds*
Large pinch of celery salt	*Large pinch of celery salt*
Large pinch of freshly ground black pepper	*Large pinch of freshly ground black pepper*

Put the cabbage and carrots in a salad bowl. Place the remaining ingredients in a screw-topped jar and shake vigorously. Add to the cabbage and carrot mixture and toss thoroughly.

Potato salad

Metric	Imperial
500 g waxy potatoes, cooked, peeled and sliced	*1 lb waxy potatoes, cooked, peeled and sliced*
120 ml mayonnaise	*4 fl oz mayonnaise*
1 × 15 ml spoon lemon juice	*1 tablespoon lemon juice*
1 × 15 ml spoon olive oil	*1 tablespoon olive oil*
1 × 2.5 ml spoon salt	*½ teaspoon salt*
1 × 2.5 ml spoon freshly ground black pepper	*½ teaspoon freshly ground black pepper*
2 × 15 ml spoons finely chopped fresh chives	*2 tablespoons finely chopped fresh chives*
4 × 15 ml spoons finely chopped leeks	*4 tablespoons finely chopped leeks*

Place the potatoes in a mixing bowl. Mix together the mayonnaise, lemon juice, oil, salt, pepper and 1 × 15 ml spoon (1 tablespoon) of the chives. Add to the potatoes and toss gently until well coated.

Spoon the mixture into a serving bowl. Sprinkle with the remaining chives and scatter the leeks around the edge of the bowl.

Cover and chill for 30 minutes before serving.

Pepper, anchovy and tomato salad

Metric	Imperial
2 large red peppers	*2 large red peppers*
3 large tomatoes, skinned, seeded and sliced	*3 large tomatoes, skinned, seeded and sliced*
2 × 50 g cans anchovy fillets, drained	*2 × 2 oz cans anchovy fillets, drained*
4 × 15 ml spoons olive oil	*4 tablespoons olive oil*
2 × 15 ml spoons lemon juice	*2 tablespoons lemon juice*
1 small garlic clove, crushed	*1 small garlic clove, crushed*
Large pinch of salt	*Large pinch of salt*
Large pinch of freshly ground black pepper	*Large pinch of freshly ground black pepper*

Place the peppers under a preheated hot grill, and cook, turning them frequently, until the skins are charred. Remove from the grill and place under cold running water – the skins will now come off easily. Remove the core and seeds and cut the flesh into wide strips.

Arrange the peppers on a flat serving dish with the sliced tomatoes.

Rinse the anchovy fillets under cold water to remove excess salt. Lay a lattice of anchovy fillets on top of the peppers and tomatoes.

Mix together the oil, lemon juice, garlic, salt and pepper. Pour this dressing over the pepper, tomato and anchovy salad. Chill for 30 minutes before serving.

Coleslaw with Italian dressing (top); Potato salad; Pepper, anchovy and tomato salad

MAIN MEAL SALADS

Salade niçoise

Metric

1 small lettuce, separated
into leaves
6 medium potatoes,
cooked, peeled and diced
350 g French beans, cut
into 2.5 cm lengths and
cooked
6 tomatoes, skinned and
quartered
120 ml French dressing
1 × 200 g can tuna fish,
drained and flaked into
bite-size pieces

To garnish:
6 anchovy fillets, halved
10 black olives, stoned
2 × 15 ml spoons capers

Imperial

1 small lettuce, separated
into leaves
6 medium potatoes,
cooked, peeled and diced
12 oz French beans, cut
into 1 inch lengths and
cooked
6 tomatoes, skinned and
quartered
4 fl oz French dressing
1 × 7 oz can tuna fish,
drained and flaked into
bite-size pieces

To garnish:
6 anchovy fillets, halved
10 black olives, stoned
2 tablespoons capers

Arrange the lettuce leaves on a large, shallow serving dish.
Mix together the potatoes, beans, tomatoes, French
dressing and tuna and toss gently to combine. Spoon the
mixture onto the lettuce leaves and garnish with the
anchovy fillets, olives and capers. Serve at once.
Serves 6

Greek rice ring

Metric

225 g long-grain rice
Salt
Lemon juice
2 large ripe tomatoes,
skinned and chopped
4 × 5 ml spoons finely
chopped fresh chives
4 × 5 ml spoons finely
chopped fresh parsley
8 green olives, stoned and
finely chopped
1 × 2.5 ml spoon dried
marjoram
1 × 2.5 ml spoon dried
basil
1 red pepper
4 × 15 ml spoons olive oil
2 × 15 ml spoons tarragon
vinegar
Freshly ground black
pepper
Black olives to garnish

Imperial

8 oz long-grain rice
Salt
Lemon juice
2 large ripe tomatoes,
skinned and chopped
4 teaspoons finely
chopped fresh chives
4 teaspoons finely
chopped fresh parsley
8 green olives, stoned and
finely chopped
½ teaspoon dried
marjoram
½ teaspoon dried
basil
1 red pepper
4 tablespoons olive oil
2 tablespoons tarragon
vinegar
Freshly ground black
pepper
Black olives to garnish

Cook the rice in boiling salted water, with 1 × 5 ml spoon
(1 teaspoon) lemon juice, for about 15 minutes or until just
tender. Drain in a colander.
Meanwhile, put the tomatoes in a large bowl with the
chives, parsley, green olives, marjoram and basil. Blanch
the pepper in boiling water for 5 minutes, then drain and
remove the core and seeds. Cut into narrow strips. Add to
the tomato mixture with the warm rice.
Put the oil, vinegar and salt and black pepper to taste in a
screw-topped jar and shake well to mix. Add enough of this
to moisten the rice mixture, adjust the seasoning and
sharpen with lemon juice. Press this mixture firmly into a
small ring mould and chill for 1 hour.
Invert onto a serving dish and garnish with black olives.
Serve with cooked chicken, scampi or lobster. Alternatively,
serve the rice ring hot: cover the mould with buttered foil
and place it in a roasting tin containing about 1 cm (½ inch)
boiling water. Heat on the top of the stove for 15 to 20
minutes. Remove the foil, invert the rice ring onto a
serving dish and garnish with black olives. Serve with
kebabs or grilled poultry.
Serves 6

Midsummer salad

Metric	Imperial
250 ml double cream	8 fl oz double cream
1 × 5 ml spoon lemon juice	1 teaspoon lemon juice
50 g button mushrooms, thinly sliced	2 oz button mushrooms, thinly sliced
4 small carrots, peeled and grated	4 small carrots, peeled and grated
Large pinch of salt	Large pinch of salt
Large pinch of freshly ground black pepper	Large pinch of freshly ground black pepper
Large pinch of grated nutmeg	Large pinch of grated nutmeg
1 bunch of watercress	1 bunch of watercress
½ cucumber, thinly sliced	½ cucumber, thinly sliced
350 g cold cooked meat or poultry, thinly sliced	12 oz cold cooked meat or poultry, thinly sliced
1 small lettuce, shredded	1 small lettuce, shredded

Mix the cream with the lemon juice, and fold in the mushrooms and grated carrots. Season with the salt, pepper and nutmeg. Pile this mixture into the centre of a shallow serving dish and surround it with rings of watercress, cucumber and meat or poultry. Finish with a ring of lettuce. Chill for 20 minutes before serving.

Russian salad

Metric	Imperial
3 large potatoes, cooked, peeled and diced	3 large potatoes, cooked, peeled and diced
4 medium carrots, peeled, cooked and diced	4 medium carrots, peeled, cooked and diced
100 g French beans, cooked and halved	4 oz French beans, cooked and halved
1 small onion, peeled and very finely chopped	1 small onion, peeled and very finely chopped
100 g peas, cooked	4 oz peas, cooked
50 g cooked tongue, diced	2 oz cooked tongue, diced
100 g cooked chicken, diced	4 oz cooked chicken, diced
50 g garlic sausage, diced	2 oz garlic sausage, diced
250 ml mayonnaise	8 fl oz mayonnaise
Large pinch of cayenne pepper	Large pinch of cayenne pepper
2 hard-boiled eggs, sliced, to garnish	2 hard-boiled eggs, sliced, to garnish

Put the potatoes, carrots, beans, onion, peas, tongue, chicken and sausage in a salad bowl. Mix together the mayonnaise and cayenne and add to the bowl. Toss well. Garnish with the eggs and chill for about 20 minutes before serving.

Midsummer salad (behind); Wurst salat (left); Russian salad

Wurst salat

Metric

500 g mixed cooked
German wurst, sliced
1 medium green pepper,
cored, seeded and sliced
1 medium red pepper,
cored, seeded and sliced
1 onion, peeled and thinly
sliced into rings
120 ml French dressing
2 small pickled gherkins,
halved

Imperial

1 lb mixed cooked
German wurst, sliced
1 medium green pepper,
cored, seeded and sliced
1 medium red pepper,
cored, seeded and sliced
1 onion, peeled and thinly
sliced into rings
4 fl oz French dressing
2 small pickled gherkins,
halved

Arrange the wurst and green and red peppers decoratively
on a serving plate. Scatter over the onion rings. Pour over
the French dressing and garnish with the gherkin halves.
Chill for about 30 minutes before serving.

Clockwise: Rice and avocado salad (top); Ox tongue and orange salad; Broad bean and ham salad; Carrot and fruit salad

Carrot and fruit salad

Metric	Imperial
4 medium carrots, peeled and grated	*4 medium carrots, peeled and grated*
1 medium eating apple, peeled, cored and finely chopped	*1 medium eating apple, peeled, cored and finely chopped*
1 small orange, peeled, pith removed and finely chopped	*1 small orange, peeled, pith removed and finely chopped*
2 × 15 ml spoons lemon juice	*2 tablespoons lemon juice*
50 g cream cheese	*2 oz cream cheese*
1 × 15 ml spoon finely chopped fresh parsley	*1 tablespoon finely chopped fresh parsley*
1 × 2.5 ml spoon salt	*½ teaspoon salt*
Large pinch of white pepper	*Large pinch of white pepper*
Large pinch of paprika	*Large pinch of paprika*

Combine the carrots, apple, orange and 1 × 15 ml spoon (1 tablespoon) of the lemon juice in a mixing bowl. Chill for 30 minutes.

Mix the cream cheese and the remaining lemon juice together with a fork. Stir in the parsley, salt, pepper and paprika.

Stir the cream cheese mixture into the salad and serve at once.

28

Rice and avocado salad

Metric

120 ml French dressing
1 garlic clove
225 g long-grain rice
2 avocados, peeled,
stoned and cubed
3 medium tomatoes,
skinned, seeded and
chopped
2 hard-boiled eggs,
chopped
50 g mushrooms, sliced

Imperial

4 fl oz French dressing
1 garlic clove
8 oz long-grain rice
2 avocados, peeled,
stoned and cubed
3 medium tomatoes,
skinned, seeded and
chopped
2 hard-boiled eggs,
chopped
2 oz mushrooms, sliced

Put the French dressing in a screw-topped jar and add the garlic clove. Leave for 1 hour. Meanwhile, cook the rice in plenty of boiling salted water for 15 minutes or until it is tender. Drain well and allow to cool.

Put the rice in a salad bowl and add the avocados, tomatoes, eggs and mushrooms.

Remove the garlic clove from the dressing and discard. Pour the dressing over the rice mixture. Stir well. Chill for 1 hour, stirring occasionally. Serve chilled.

Ox tongue and orange salad

Metric

500 g cooked ox tongue,
diced
1 × 2.5 ml spoon salt
Large pinch of freshly
ground black pepper
4 × 15 ml spoons olive oil
4 × 15 ml spoons orange
juice
1 × 15 ml spoon finely
grated lemon rind
4 × 15 ml spoons lemon
juice
1 × 15 ml spoon capers
6 oranges, peeled, pith
removed and segmented
2 heads of chicory,
separated into leaves

Imperial

1 lb cooked ox tongue,
diced
½ teaspoon salt
Large pinch of freshly
ground black pepper
4 tablespoons olive oil
4 tablespoons orange
juice
1 tablespoon finely
grated lemon rind
4 tablespoons lemon
juice
1 tablespoon capers
6 oranges, peeled, pith
removed and segmented
2 heads of chicory,
separated into leaves

Place the ox tongue in a mixing bowl and add the salt, pepper and 1 × 15 ml spoon (1 tablespoon) of the oil. Mix well.

Add the orange juice, grated lemon rind, lemon juice and capers to the remaining oil and mix well. Add the orange segments and orange juice mixture to the ox tongue and stir to mix.

Line the edge of a shallow serving dish with the chicory leaves. Pile the ox tongue and orange mixture in the centre. Serve immediately.

Serves 6

Broad bean and ham salad

Metric

175 g thick cut cooked
ham, cubed
1 × 15 ml spoon Worcestershire sauce
500 g broad beans, podded
150 ml soured cream
1 × 5 ml spoon chopped
fresh chives
Large pinch of paprika
1 × 2.5 ml spoon salt
Large pinch of freshly
ground black pepper
Few lettuce leaves
Chopped fresh chives to
garnish

Imperial

6 oz thick cut cooked
ham, cubed
1 tablespoon Worcester-
shire sauce
1 lb broad beans, podded
¼ pint soured cream
1 teaspoon chopped
fresh chives
Large pinch of paprika
½ teaspoon salt
Large pinch of freshly
ground black pepper
Few lettuce leaves
Chopped fresh chives to
garnish

Mix the ham with the Worcestershire sauce in a mixing bowl. Leave for 10 minutes.

Meanwhile, cook the beans in boiling salted water for 5 minutes. Drain and refresh under cold running water. Add to the ham with the soured cream, chives, paprika, salt and pepper. Mix well.

Line a shallow salad dish with the lettuce leaves and spoon over the bean and ham mixture. Chill for 30 minutes before serving, garnished with chives.

Salmagundy; Mussel, hake and vegetable salad; Tomato and fish salad

Tomato and fish salad

Metric

500 g mackerel fillets,
skinned, cooked and cut
into 2.5 cm pieces
200 ml lemon juice
1 × 5 ml spoon salt
1 × 5 ml spoon black
peppercorns, crushed
120 ml olive oil
6 tomatoes, skinned,
seeded and chopped
2 large onions, peeled and
thinly sliced into rings
100 g green olives, stoned
1 × 2.5 ml spoon dried
oregano
2 green chillis, seeded and
finely chopped
175 ml dry white wine
1 avocado, halved,
stoned, peeled and
thinly sliced

Imperial

1 lb mackerel fillets,
skinned, cooked and cut
into 1 inch pieces
⅓ pint lemon juice
1 teaspoon salt
1 teaspoon black
peppercorns, crushed
4 fl oz olive oil
6 tomatoes, skinned,
seeded and chopped
2 large onions, peeled and
thinly sliced into rings
4 oz green olives, stoned
½ teaspoon dried
oregano
2 green chillis, seeded and
finely chopped
6 fl oz dry white wine
1 avocado, halved,
stoned, peeled and
thinly sliced

Place the mackerel in a shallow serving dish and pour over the lemon juice. Sprinkle over the salt and peppercorns and leave in the refrigerator for at least 4 hours.

Mix together the oil, tomatoes, onions, olives, oregano, chillis and wine.

Drain off and discard the lemon juice from the fish and pour over the oil and wine mixture. Chill for about 30 minutes before serving, garnished with the avocado slices.

Mussel, hake and vegetable salad

Metric	Imperial
120 ml olive oil	*4 fl oz olive oil*
Large pinch of hot chilli powder	*Large pinch of hot chilli powder*
2 × 15 ml spoons finely chopped fresh parsley	*2 tablespoons finely chopped fresh parsley*
Large pinch of dried thyme	*Large pinch of dried thyme*
1 bay leaf	*1 bay leaf*
2 garlic cloves, crushed	*2 garlic cloves, crushed*
750 g hake, cut into 6 × 2.5 cm wide slices	*1½ lb hake, cut into 6 × 1 inch wide slices*
100 g frozen petits pois, cooked	*4 oz frozen petits pois, cooked*
2 canned red pimientos, drained and cut into strips	*2 canned red pimientos, drained and cut into strips*
24 mussels, scrubbed, steamed and removed from the shells	*24 mussels, scrubbed, steamed and removed from the shells*
4 mussels, scrubbed and steamed open, to garnish	*4 mussels, scrubbed and steamed open, to garnish*

Cooking time: 25 minutes
Oven: 190°C, 375°F, Gas Mark 5

Mix together the oil, chilli powder, parsley, thyme, bay leaf and garlic in a shallow ovenproof dish. Place the fish in the dish in one layer and leave to marinate at room temperature for 1 hour, basting occasionally.

Cover the dish tightly and bake in a preheated moderately hot oven for 15 minutes.

Remove the dish from the oven. Uncover and add the petits pois, pimientos and mussels. Return to the oven and cook for a further 5 to 10 minutes or until the fish flakes easily when tested with a fork.

Remove the dish from the oven. Remove and discard the bay leaf. Garnish with the mussels on their shells. Allow to cool, then chill in the refrigerator for 1 hour. Serve chilled.

Salmagundy

Metric	Imperial
500 g cooked chicken, sliced	*1 lb cooked chicken, sliced*
500 g lean cooked tongue, sliced	*1 lb lean cooked tongue, sliced*
4 rollmops or pickled herrings, drained	*4 rollmops or pickled herrings, drained*
2 large tomatoes, skinned and quartered	*2 large tomatoes, skinned and quartered*
1 large orange, cut into 8 sections	*1 large orange, cut into 8 sections*
Watercress to garnish	*Watercress to garnish*

Arrange the chicken slices around the edge of a serving plate and then, inside the chicken circle, make another slightly smaller circle with the tongue. Arrange the rollmops or herrings on the meat and place a tomato quarter between each herring. Add the orange quarters and garnish with watercress.

Serves 8 to 10

Greek salad

Metric	Imperial
1 Cos lettuce	*1 Cos lettuce*
1 bunch of radishes, sliced	*1 bunch of radishes, sliced*
225 g feta cheese, cut into cubes	*8 oz feta cheese, cut into cubes*
Large pinch of dried marjoram	*Large pinch of dried marjoram*
4 tomatoes, skinned and sliced	*4 tomatoes, skinned and sliced*
6 anchovy fillets, finely chopped	*6 anchovy fillets, finely chopped*
6 large black olives, halved and stoned	*6 large black olives, halved and stoned*
1 × 15 ml spoon finely chopped fresh parsley	*1 tablespoon finely chopped fresh parsley*
1 × 2.5 ml spoon freshly ground black pepper	*½ teaspoon freshly ground black pepper*

Dressing:	Dressing:
4 × 15 ml spoons olive oil	*4 tablespoons olive oil*
4 × 5 ml spoons white wine vinegar	*4 teaspoons white wine vinegar*
1 × 15 ml spoon finely chopped fresh mixed herbs	*1 tablespoon finely chopped fresh mixed herbs*
4 spring onions, chopped	*4 spring onions, chopped*
1 × 5 ml spoon sugar	*1 teaspoon sugar*
Large pinch of salt	*Large pinch of salt*
1 × 2.5 ml spoon freshly ground black pepper	*½ teaspoon freshly ground black pepper*

Tear the lettuce into pieces and arrange on a large dish. Scatter the radish slices over the lettuce. Pile the cheese in the centre of the dish and sprinkle with the marjoram. Place the tomatoes in a circle around the cheese and place the anchovies on top of the tomatoes, alternating with the olives. Sprinkle with the parsley and black pepper.
Mix together the dressing ingredients in a screw-topped jar. Pour the dressing over the salad and serve.

Chicken and apple salad

Metric	Imperial
1 × 275 g can potatoes, drained and thickly sliced	*1 × 10 oz can potatoes, drained and thickly sliced*
4 × 15 ml spoons olive oil	*4 tablespoons olive oil*
350 g cooked chicken, diced	*12 oz cooked chicken, diced*
2 red eating apples, cored and sliced	*2 red eating apples, cored and sliced*
100 g cooked ham, diced	*4 oz cooked ham, diced*
1 × 5 ml spoon dried mixed herbs	*1 teaspoon dried mixed herbs*
2 × 15 ml spoons lemon juice	*2 tablespoons lemon juice*
1 × 2.5 ml spoon salt	*½ teaspoon salt*
Large pinch of freshly ground black pepper	*Large pinch of freshly ground black pepper*
1 small Cos lettuce, separated into leaves	*1 small Cos lettuce, separated into leaves*
Paprika	*Paprika*

Put the potatoes in a mixing bowl. Add the oil and toss to coat. Add the chicken, apples, ham, herbs, lemon juice, salt and pepper. Toss thoroughly and chill for 30 minutes. Arrange the lettuce on a shallow serving dish. Pile the chicken mixture in the centre and sprinkle with paprika.

Chicken and apple salad; Greek salad; Potato, beef and tomato salad

Potato, beef and tomato salad

Metric

*1 small lettuce,
separated into leaves
1 kg cold roast beef, cubed
4 medium potatoes,
cooked, peeled and cubed
4 medium tomatoes,
skinned, seeded and
quartered
4 pickled gherkins, sliced*

Sauce:
*350 ml soured cream
3 × 15 ml spoons
horseradish sauce
1 × 2.5 ml spoon salt
1 × 2.5 ml spoon white
pepper*

To garnish:
*2 hard-boiled eggs,
thinly sliced*

Imperial

*1 small lettuce,
separated into leaves
2 lb cold roast beef, cubed
4 medium potatoes,
cooked, peeled and cubed
4 medium tomatoes,
skinned, seeded and
quartered
4 pickled gherkins, sliced*

Sauce:
*12 fl oz soured cream
3 tablespoons
horseradish sauce
½ teaspoon salt
½ teaspoon white
pepper*

To garnish:
*2 hard-boiled eggs,
thinly sliced*

Arrange the lettuce leaves on a large, shallow serving plate. Put the meat, potatoes, tomatoes and gherkins in a mixing bowl. Mix together the ingredients for the sauce. Add to the meat mixture and toss gently.
Pile the meat mixture on the lettuce leaves. Garnish with the egg slices and serve at once.

North African salad

Metric	Imperial
175 g long-grain rice	6 oz long-grain rice
1 small cucumber, sliced	1 small cucumber, sliced
2 medium bananas, peeled and sliced	2 medium bananas, peeled and sliced
2 × 15 ml spoons seedless raisins	2 tablespoons seedless raisins
1 × 15 ml spoon chopped almonds	1 tablespoon chopped almonds
4 × 15 ml spoons olive oil	4 tablespoons olive oil
4 × 5 ml spoons lemon juice	4 teaspoons lemon juice
1 × 15 ml spoon grated lemon rind	1 tablespoon grated lemon rind
1 × 5 ml spoon salt	1 teaspoon salt
Large pinch of ground coriander	Large pinch of ground coriander
Large pinch of ground cumin	Large pinch of ground cumin
Large pinch of cayenne pepper	Large pinch of cayenne pepper
1 × 5 ml spoon clear honey	1 teaspoon clear honey

Cook the rice in boiling salted water for 15 minutes or until it is tender. Drain well and allow to cool.

Put the rice, cucumber, bananas, raisins and almonds in a salad bowl and stir well.

Mix together the oil, lemon juice and rind, salt, coriander, cumin, cayenne and honey in a screw-topped jar. Pour the dressing over the rice mixture and mix well. Chill for 30 minutes before serving.

Creole banana salad

Metric	Imperial
225 g long-grain rice	8 oz long-grain rice
4 large bananas, peeled and sliced	4 large bananas, peeled and sliced
1 × 15 ml spoon lemon juice	1 tablespoon lemon juice
1 medium red eating apple, cored and chopped	1 medium red eating apple, cored and chopped
100 g seedless green grapes	4 oz seedless green grapes
75 g canned or fresh pineapple, chopped	3 oz canned or fresh pineapple, chopped
2 × 15 ml spoons finely chopped walnuts	2 tablespoons finely chopped walnuts
1 × 15 ml spoon sultanas	1 tablespoon sultanas
4 large lettuce leaves	4 large lettuce leaves
2 × 15 ml spoons desiccated coconut	2 tablespoons desiccated coconut

Dressing:

Metric	Imperial
120 ml mayonnaise	4 fl oz mayonnaise
2 × 15 ml spoons lemon juice	2 tablespoons lemon juice
Large pinch of hot chilli powder	Large pinch of hot chilli powder
1 × 2.5 ml spoon dry English mustard	½ teaspoon dry English mustard

Cook the rice in boiling salted water for 15 minutes or until it is tender. Drain well and allow to cool.

Put the rice in a mixing bowl and stir in the bananas, lemon juice, apple, grapes, pineapple, walnuts and sultanas. Mix together the mayonnaise, lemon juice, chilli powder and mustard and stir into the banana and rice mixture.

Arrange the lettuce leaves in a large serving dish. Pile the banana and rice mixture on top and sprinkle over the coconut. Serve at once.

North African salad; Nun's salad; Creole banana salad

Nun's salad

Metric

*500 g cooked chicken,
cubed*
*12 spring onions, white
part only, chopped*
*500 g potatoes, peeled,
cooked and diced*
50 g seedless raisins
*225 g large black grapes,
halved and seeded*
*50 g large black olives,
halved and stoned*
1 × 2.5 ml spoon salt
*Large pinch of freshly
ground black pepper*
*1 large eating apple,
peeled, cored and diced*
175 ml mayonnaise

Imperial

*1 lb cooked chicken,
cubed*
*12 spring onions, white
part only, chopped*
*1 lb potatoes, peeled,
cooked and diced*
2 oz seedless raisins
*8 oz large black grapes,
halved and seeded*
*2 oz large black olives,
halved and stoned*
½ teaspoon salt
*Large pinch of freshly
ground black pepper*
*1 large eating apple,
peeled, cored and diced*
6 fl oz mayonnaise

Combine the chicken, spring onions, potatoes, raisins, half the grapes, the olives, salt, pepper and apple in a large salad bowl. Pour over the mayonnaise and toss gently but thoroughly.

Arrange the remaining grape halves decoratively over the top. Chill for 30 minutes before serving.

SALAD DRESSINGS

Tomato juice dressing

Metric

300 ml tomato juice
1 × 15 ml spoon tarragon vinegar
1 garlic clove, crushed (optional)
Salt
Freshly ground black pepper

Imperial

½ pint tomato juice
1 tablespoon tarragon vinegar
1 garlic clove, crushed (optional)
Salt
Freshly ground black pepper

Shake together the tomato juice, tarragon vinegar and garlic, if used, in a screw-topped jar. Season to taste with salt and pepper. Chill before use.
Makes 300 ml (½ pint)

French dressing

Metric

2 × 15 ml spoons wine vinegar
1 × 5 ml spoon salt
1 × 5 ml spoon freshly ground black pepper
6 × 15 ml spoons olive oil

Imperial

2 tablespoons wine vinegar
1 teaspoon salt
1 teaspoon freshly ground black pepper
6 tablespoons olive oil

Put the vinegar, salt, pepper and oil in a screw-topped jar. Shake vigorously until well mixed.
Used as required.
Makes 120 ml (4 fl oz)

Tomato juice dressing; French dressing

Honey and vinegar dressing

Metric

*1 × 15 ml spoon clear
honey
150 ml vinegar
1 × 2.5 ml spoon salt
Large pinch of freshly
ground black pepper
1 × 5 ml spoon finely
chopped fresh chives*

Imperial

*1 tablespoon clear
honey
¼ pint vinegar
½ teaspoon salt
Large pinch of freshly
ground black pepper
1 teaspoon finely
chopped fresh chives*

Place all the ingredients in a screw-topped jar and shake
well. Use as required.
Makes 150 ml (¼ pint)

Mint dressing

Metric

*3 × 15 ml spoons olive oil
1 × 15 ml spoon lemon
juice
1 × 2.5 ml spoon salt
1 × 2.5 ml spoon freshly
ground black pepper
1 × 15 ml spoon finely
chopped fresh mint
2 × 5 ml spoons sugar*

Imperial

*3 tablespoons olive oil
1 tablespoon lemon
juice
½ teaspoon salt
½ teaspoon freshly
ground black pepper
1 tablespoon finely
chopped fresh mint
2 teaspoons sugar*

Put all the ingredients in a screw-topped jar and shake
well. Chill for at least 30 minutes before serving.
Makes 4 × 15 ml spoons (4 tablespoons)

Honey and vinegar dressing; Mint dressing

Yogurt dressing

Metric	Imperial
350 ml plain unsweetened yogurt	12 fl oz plain unsweetened yogurt
4 × 15 ml spoons lemon juice	4 tablespoons lemon juice
1 garlic clove, crushed	1 garlic clove, crushed
1 × 5 ml spoon salt	1 teaspoon salt
1 × 5 ml spoon freshly ground black pepper	1 teaspoon freshly ground black pepper

Place all the dressing ingredients in a mixing bowl and beat together until thoroughly combined. Use at once.
Makes 350 ml (12 fl oz)

Horseradish and soured cream dressing

Metric	Imperial
4 × 15 ml spoons grated fresh horseradish	4 tablespoons grated fresh horseradish
1 × 15 ml spoon vinegar	1 tablespoon vinegar
150 ml soured cream	¼ pint soured cream
1 × 5 ml spoon sugar	1 teaspoon sugar
Large pinch of salt	Large pinch of salt
Pinch of cayenne pepper	Pinch of cayenne pepper

Combine the horseradish, vinegar, soured cream, sugar, salt and cayenne. Chill until required.
Makes 250 ml (8 fl oz)

Roquefort dressing

Metric	Imperial
175 ml olive oil	6 fl oz olive oil
2 × 5 ml spoons salt	2 teaspoons salt
2 × 5 ml spoons freshly ground black pepper	2 teaspoons freshly ground black pepper
4 × 15 ml spoons wine vinegar	4 tablespoons wine vinegar
50 g Roquefort cheese, finely crumbled	2 oz Roquefort cheese, finely crumbled
2 × 15 ml spoons chopped fresh chives	2 tablespoons chopped fresh chives

Beat the oil, salt and pepper together in a mixing bowl. Gradually beat in the vinegar, then mash in the cheese until the mixture is thoroughly combined. Stir in the chives.
Either use the dressing immediately or pour it into a screw-topped jar and chill in the refrigerator until required.
Makes 250 ml (8 fl oz)

Blue cheese dressing

Metric	Imperial
100 g blue cheese (Stilton, Danish Blue, Dolcelatte, etc), crumbled	4 oz blue cheese (Stilton, Danish Blue, Dolcelatte, etc), crumbled
100 ml mayonnaise	4 fl oz mayonnaise
100 ml double cream	4 fl oz double cream
Large pinch of salt	Large pinch of salt
1 × 2.5 ml spoon freshly ground black pepper	½ teaspoon freshly ground black pepper

Combine all the ingredients in a mixing bowl, beating until thoroughly mixed. Store the dressing in the refrigerator until required.
Makes 300 ml (½ pint)

Clockwise: Yogurt dressing (top left); Horseradish and soured cream dressing; Roquefort dressing; Blue cheese dressing

Mayonnaise

Metric	Imperial
2 egg yolks, at room temperature	*2 egg yolks, at room temperature*
1 × 2.5 ml spoon salt	*½ teaspoon salt*
1 × 2.5 ml spoon dry mustard	*½ teaspoon dry mustard*
Pinch of freshly ground white pepper	*Pinch of freshly ground white pepper*
300 ml olive oil, at room temperature	*½ pint olive oil, at room temperature*
1 × 15 ml spoon white wine vinegar or lemon juice	*1 tablespoon white wine vinegar or lemon juice*

Place the egg yolks, salt, mustard and pepper in a mixing bowl. Beat until well mixed and slightly thickened. Add the oil a few drops at a time, beating constantly. (Do not add the oil too quickly or the mayonnaise will curdle.) After the mixture has thickened the oil may be added in a thin stream.

Beat in a few drops of vinegar or lemon juice from time to time to prevent the mayonnaise from becoming too thick. When all of the oil has been added, stir in the remaining wine vinegar or lemon juice.

Taste the sauce for seasoning and add more salt, mustard and wine vinegar if desired.

Makes 300 ml (½ pint)

Egg and caper dressing

Metric	Imperial
3 hard-boiled egg yolks	*3 hard-boiled egg yolks*
2 × 5 ml spoons prepared French mustard	*2 teaspoons prepared French mustard*
1 small garlic clove, crushed	*1 small garlic clove, crushed*
1 × 2.5 ml spoon salt	*½ teaspoon salt*
Large pinch of freshly ground black pepper	*Large pinch of freshly ground black pepper*
Pinch of dill seed	*Pinch of dill seed*
2 × 15 ml spoons olive oil	*2 tablespoons olive oil*
1.5 × 5 ml spoons white wine vinegar	*1½ teaspoons white wine vinegar*
2 × 15 ml spoons lemon juice	*2 tablespoons lemon juice*
1.5 × 5 ml spoons finely chopped capers	*1½ teaspoons finely chopped capers*

Put all the ingredients in a screw-topped jar and shake vigorously until well mixed. Use as required, storing in the refrigerator.

Makes 250 ml (8 fl oz)

Fines herbes vinaigrette

Metric

1 × 2.5 ml spoon finely
chopped fresh chervil
1 × 5 ml spoon finely
chopped fresh chives
1 × 15 ml spoon finely
chopped fresh parsley
1 × 5 ml spoon prepared
French mustard
1 × 2.5 ml spoon salt
Large pinch of freshly
ground black pepper
1 garlic clove, crushed
175 ml olive oil
4 × 15 ml spoons
tarragon vinegar
2 × 5 ml spoons lemon
juice

Imperial

½ teaspoon finely
chopped fresh chervil
1 teaspoon finely
chopped fresh chives
1 tablespoon finely
chopped fresh parsley
1 teaspoon prepared
French mustard
½ teaspoon salt
Large pinch of freshly
ground black pepper
1 garlic clove, crushed
6 fl oz olive oil
4 tablespoons
tarragon vinegar
2 teaspoons lemon
juice

Rub the egg yolks through a fine sieve into a small mixing bowl. Add the mustard, garlic, salt, pepper and dill and beat briskly until the mixture forms a smooth paste. Stir in the oil, a little at a time, then add the vinegar and lemon juice. Mix well and stir in the capers.
Chill for 30 minutes and serve as required.
Makes 100 ml (3 fl oz)

Egg and caper dressing; Mayonnaise; Fines herbes vinaigrette

Thousand island dressing

Metric

450 ml mayonnaise
1 × 5 ml spoon Tabasco
2 × 15 ml spoons finely
chopped pimientos or
sweet pickle
10 stuffed green olives,
finely chopped
2 hard-boiled eggs,
very finely chopped
1 medium shallot,
peeled and very finely
chopped
3 × 15 ml spoons olive oil
1 × 2.5 ml spoon salt
1 × 2.5 spoon freshly
ground black pepper
1 × 15 ml spoon wine
vinegar

Imperial

¾ pint mayonnaise
1 teaspoon Tabasco
2 tablespoons finely
chopped pimientos or
sweet pickle
10 stuffed green olives,
finely chopped
2 hard-boiled eggs,
very finely chopped
1 medium shallot,
peeled and very finely
chopped
3 tablespoons olive oil
½ teaspoon salt
½ teaspoon freshly
ground black pepper
1 tablespoon wine
vinegar

Mix together all the ingredients. Pour into a serving bowl
and chill for at least 1 hour before serving.
Makes 600 ml (1 pint)

Thousand island dressing; Cucumber mousse with ham

SPECIAL OCCASION SALADS

Cucumber mousse with ham

Metric

½ packet lemon-flavoured jelly
150 ml boiling water
1 cucumber
Salt
2 × 225 g cartons cottage cheese
150 ml mayonnaise or soured cream
6 × 15 ml spoons cold water
15 g powdered gelatine
Freshly ground white pepper
Lemon juice or wine vinegar
8 slices of cooked ham, rolled

Imperial

½ packet lemon-flavoured jelly
¼ pint boiling water
1 cucumber
Salt
2 × 8 oz cartons cottage cheese
¼ pint mayonnaise or soured cream
6 tablespoons cold water
½ oz powdered gelatine
Freshly ground white pepper
Lemon juice or wine vinegar
8 slices of cooked ham, rolled

Dissolve the jelly in the boiling water and allow to cool. Make a layer of the jelly on the bottom of a 900 ml (1½ pint) ring mould. Thinly slice one quarter of the unpeeled cucumber. Quarter the slices and arrange in the jelly. Allow to set.

Peel the remaining cucumber, cut in half lengthways and remove the seeds. Chop the flesh and place in a colander. Sprinkle with salt and leave for 1 hour to draw the juices. Rinse and drain well, then pat dry with absorbent kitchen paper.

Press the cottage cheese through a fine sieve into a mixing bowl. Stir in the mayonnaise or soured cream.

Place the cold water in a small saucepan. Sprinkle over the gelatine. Allow to soak for a few minutes, then stir over a low heat until the gelatine has dissolved. Cool slightly, then stir into the cottage cheese mixture. Add salt, pepper and lemon juice or wine vinegar to taste. Fold in the chopped cucumber. When the mixture begins to set, pour into the ring mould on top of the jelly mixture. Chill until set.

To turn out of the mould, dip into hot water for 15 seconds, then invert quickly onto a serving dish. Arrange the rolled slices of ham in the centre.

Serves 4 to 6

Kartoffel salat

Metric	Imperial
1 kg waxy potatoes	*2 lb waxy potatoes*
1 × 5 ml spoon salt	*1 teaspoon salt*
6 lettuce leaves	*6 lettuce leaves*
4 tomatoes, skinned and quartered	*4 tomatoes, skinned and quartered*
2 × 15 ml spoons salted cashew nuts	*2 tablespoons salted cashew nuts*
2 × 15 ml spoons finely chopped fresh mint or parsley	*2 tablespoons finely chopped fresh mint or parsley*

Dressing:

Metric	Imperial
3 × 15 ml spoons cider vinegar	*3 tablespoons cider vinegar*
120 ml olive oil	*4 fl oz olive oil*
1 × 15 ml spoon prepared mild French mustard	*1 tablespoon prepared mild French mustard*
1 × 2.5 ml spoon salt	*½ teaspoon salt*
Large pinch of freshly ground black pepper	*Large pinch of freshly ground black pepper*
3 × 15 ml spoons finely chopped spring onions	*3 tablespoons finely chopped spring onions*

Place the potatoes in a pan, cover with water, add the salt and bring to the boil. Reduce the heat to moderate and cook for 15 to 20 minutes or until the potatoes are cooked. Drain, peel and slice thickly into a mixing bowl. Leave to cool slightly.

Meanwhile, prepare the dressing. Put all the ingredients in a screw-topped jar and shake until well mixed. Pour the dressing over the warm potato slices and toss gently until they become well coated. Chill for 30 minutes.

Arrange the lettuce leaves in a salad bowl. Spoon the potato slices into the centre and arrange the tomato quarters around the sides. Sprinkle over the nuts and mint before serving.

Kartoffel salat; Crabmeat salad

Crabmeat salad

Metric

500 g cooked crabmeat
1 large Webb lettuce,
separated into leaves
4 firm tomatoes, skinned
and sliced
1 avocado, peeled, stoned,
sliced and gently rubbed
with lemon juice
½ cucumber, thinly sliced
9 black olives, stoned

Rémoulade sauce:
300 ml mayonnaise
1 × 5 ml spoon anchovy
essence
1 × 2.5 ml spoon finely
chopped fresh parsley
1.5 × 5 ml spoons capers
(optional)
1 hard-boiled egg,
chopped
1 garlic clove, crushed
1 × 5 ml spoon finely
chopped fresh tarragon

Imperial

1 lb cooked crabmeat
1 large Webb lettuce,
separated into leaves
4 firm tomatoes, skinned
and sliced
1 avocado, peeled, stoned,
sliced and gently rubbed
with lemon juice
½ cucumber, thinly sliced
9 black olives, stoned

Rémoulade sauce:
½ pint mayonnaise
1 teaspoon anchovy
essence
½ teaspoon finely
chopped fresh parsley
1½ teaspoons capers
(optional)
1 hard-boiled egg,
chopped
1 garlic clove, crushed
1 teaspoon finely
chopped fresh tarragon

Mix together the ingredients for the rémoulade sauce. Remove any shell and cartilage from the crabmeat and flake the fish.
Arrange the lettuce leaves on a large serving dish. Put the crabmeat in the centre of the dish and arrange the tomatoes, avocado, cucumber and olives around the crabmeat. Pour over the sauce and serve at once.

Shellfish mayonnaise

Metric	Imperial
3 fresh scallops, cleaned and opened, or frozen scallops	3 fresh scallops, cleaned and opened, or frozen scallops
25 g butter	1 oz butter
175 g jar mussels, drained	6 oz jar mussels, drained
175 g peeled prawns	6 oz peeled prawns
175 g cooked crabmeat	6 oz cooked crabmeat
300 ml mayonnaise	½ pint mayonnaise
2 × 15 ml spoons tomato juice	2 tablespoons tomato juice
Salt	Salt
Freshly ground white pepper	Freshly ground white pepper
To garnish:	To garnish:
Watercress	Watercress
Finely chopped fresh parsley	Finely chopped fresh parsley
Lemon slices	Lemon slices

Remove the beard from the scallops and carefully wash the white flesh and bright orange roe. Replace in the shells and dot with the butter. Bake in a preheated moderately hot oven (190°C, 375°F, Gas Mark 5) for 10 minutes. Cool, then remove from the shells and chop roughly. (If using frozen scallops, cook according to the directions on the packet.)

Rinse the mussels under cold water to remove any excess brine. Mix with the scallops and prawns. Remove any shell and cartilage from the crabmeat and flake the fish. Add to the scallop mixture.

Mix together the mayonnaise and tomato juice. Season to taste with salt and pepper. Fold in the seafood.

Pile the seafood mixture on a serving dish. Garnish with watercress, chopped parsley and lemon slices.

Melon and prawn salad

Metric	Imperial
1 honeydew melon, halved, seeded and cubed	1 honeydew melon, halved, seeded and cubed
175 g peeled prawns	6 oz peeled prawns
300 ml mayonnaise	½ pint mayonnaise
2 × 15 ml spoons tomato purée	2 tablespoons tomato purée
1 × 15 ml spoon grated lemon rind	1 tablespoon grated lemon rind
1 × 5 ml spoon caster sugar	1 teaspoon caster sugar
Salt	Salt
Freshly ground white pepper	Freshly ground white pepper
Lettuce leaves	Lettuce leaves
To garnish:	To garnish:
Watercress sprigs	Watercress sprigs
Whole unpeeled prawns	Whole unpeeled prawns

Mix the melon pieces with the peeled prawns. Mix together the mayonnaise, tomato purée, lemon rind, sugar, and salt and pepper to taste. Add the melon and prawn mixture and stir to mix.

Arrange the lettuce leaves on a serving dish and pile the prawn and melon mixture in the centre. Garnish with the watercress and whole unpeeled prawns. Serve at once.

Melon and prawn salad; Shellfish mayonnaise

Pecan peach salad

Metric	Imperial
4 ripe peaches, peeled, halved and stoned	4 ripe peaches, peeled, halved and stoned
2 × 15 ml spoons lemon juice	2 tablespoons lemon juice
225 g cottage cheese	8 oz cottage cheese
100 g pecan nuts, finely chopped	4 oz pecan nuts, finely chopped
8 lettuce leaves	8 lettuce leaves

Put the peaches in a mixing bowl and sprinkle with the lemon juice. Toss so that they become well coated in the juice.

Mix together the cottage cheese and pecan nuts.

Arrange the lettuce leaves on four individual serving dishes. Place two peach halves on each dish, cut sides up. Spoon the cottage cheese mixture into the centres and serve.

Apricot and tarragon salad

Metric	Imperial
1 kg ripe apricots, peeled	2 lb ripe apricots, peeled
4 × 15 ml spoons soured cream	4 tablespoons soured cream
3 × 15 ml spoons tarragon vinegar	3 tablespoons tarragon vinegar
1 × 15 ml spoon sugar	1 tablespoon sugar
1 × 2.5 ml spoon salt	½ teaspoon salt
Large pinch of freshly ground black pepper	Large pinch of freshly ground black pepper
A few fresh tarragon leaves to garnish	A few fresh tarragon leaves to garnish

Cut each apricot in half and remove the stones. Arrange the apricots in a glass serving dish. Crack the stones with a nutcracker or hammer and take out the kernels. Chop the kernels and set aside.

To make the dressing, combine the soured cream, vinegar, sugar, salt and pepper. Pour the dressing over the apricots. Sprinkle with the tarragon leaves and chopped kernels and serve.

Apricot and tarragon salad; Pecan peach salad

Asparagus salad

Metric	Imperial
225 g asparagus, cooked, cooled and chopped	8 oz asparagus, cooked, cooled and chopped
1 small Cos lettuce, coarsely shredded	1 small Cos lettuce, coarsely shredded
4 × 15 ml spoons French dressing	4 tablespoons French dressing
1 small onion, peeled and thinly sliced into rings	1 small onion, peeled and thinly sliced into rings
1 × 15 ml spoon finely chopped fresh parsley	1 tablespoon finely chopped fresh parsley

Put the asparagus and lettuce in a mixing bowl. Pour over the French dressing and toss to coat well. Chill for about 30 minutes, turning occasionally.
Divide between four individual salad dishes and arrange the onion rings on top. Sprinkle with the chopped parsley and serve.

Brazil nut salad

Metric	Imperial
1 crisp lettuce, separated into leaves	1 crisp lettuce, separated into leaves
4 × 15 ml spoons French dressing	4 tablespoons French dressing
3 bananas, peeled and thinly sliced	3 bananas, peeled and thinly sliced
1 × 15 ml spoon lemon juice	1 tablespoon lemon juice
100 g Brazil nuts, finely chopped	4 oz Brazil nuts, finely chopped

Arrange half of the lettuce leaves in a shallow salad bowl. Shred the remaining lettuce into a mixing bowl and pour over the French dressing. Toss to coat well.
Sprinkle the bananas with the lemon juice. Add half the bananas and the Brazil nuts to the shredded lettuce and toss to combine.
Pile the nut and banana mixture on top of the lettuce leaves in the serving bowl. Arrange the remaining banana slices around the edge in a ring and serve.

Asparagus salad; Brazil nut salad

Neapolitan salad; Andalusian rice salad; Tuscan salad (behind)

Andalusian rice salad

Metric

100 g long-grain rice
1 small onion, peeled and finely chopped
2 garlic cloves, crushed
1 × 15 ml spoon finely chopped fresh parsley
6 × 15 ml spoons olive oil
1 × 15 ml spoon red wine vinegar
1 × 5 ml spoon paprika
1 × 2.5 ml spoon salt
1 × 2.5 ml spoon white pepper
500 g tomatoes, skinned and quartered
4 hard-boiled eggs, quartered
2 red peppers, cored, seeded and sliced
2 × 15 ml spoons finely chopped fresh chervil or 1 × 5 ml spoon dried chervil

Imperial

4 oz long-grain rice
1 small onion, peeled and finely chopped
2 garlic cloves, crushed
1 tablespoon finely chopped fresh parsley
6 tablespoons olive oil
1 tablespoon red wine vinegar
1 teaspoon paprika
½ teaspoon salt
½ teaspoon white pepper
1 lb tomatoes, skinned and quartered
4 hard-boiled eggs, quartered
2 red peppers, cored, seeded and sliced
2 tablespoons finely chopped fresh chervil or 1 teaspoon dried chervil

Cook the rice in boiling salted water for 15 minutes or until tender. Drain well and allow to cool.

Put the rice in a mixing bowl and stir in the onion, garlic, parsley, oil, vinegar, paprika, salt and pepper. Pile the mixture in the centre of a large serving dish.

Arrange the tomatoes, eggs and peppers decoratively around the rice and sprinkle with the chopped chervil. Serve at once.

Neapolitan salad

Metric

4 medium tomatoes, skinned and quartered
1 small green pepper, cored, seeded and thinly sliced
1 small red pepper, cored, seeded and thinly sliced
1 small lettuce, shredded
½ × 200 g can sweetcorn, drained
50 g Mozzarella cheese, chopped
3 hard-boiled eggs, quartered or sliced
3 spring onions, thinly sliced
6 black olives, halved and stoned
120 ml French dressing
1 garlic clove, finely chopped
1 × 2.5 ml spoon dried oregano
1 × 15 ml spoon finely chopped fresh basil (optional)

Imperial

4 medium tomatoes, skinned and quartered
1 small green pepper, cored, seeded and thinly sliced
1 small red pepper, cored, seeded and thinly sliced
1 small lettuce, shredded
½ × 7 oz can sweetcorn, drained
2 oz Mozzarella cheese, chopped
3 hard-boiled eggs, quartered or sliced
3 spring onions, thinly sliced
6 black olives, halved and stoned
4 fl oz French dressing
1 garlic clove, finely chopped
½ teaspoon dried oregano
1 tablespoon finely chopped fresh basil (optional)

Put the tomatoes, green and red peppers, lettuce, sweetcorn, cheese, eggs, spring onions and olives in a large salad bowl. Chill for 20 minutes.
Mix together the French dressing, garlic and oregano in a screw-topped jar and shake vigorously. Pour the dressing over the salad and toss well.
Sprinkle the chopped basil over the top, if used, and serve at once.

Tuscan salad

Metric

225 g long-grain rice
4 × 15 ml spoons dry white wine
1 green pepper, cored, seeded and thinly sliced
1 red pepper, cored, seeded and thinly sliced
1 × 100 g can fagioli, or similar small beans, drained
1 small cucumber, peeled and diced
10 stuffed green olives, halved
2 spring onions, thinly sliced

Dressing:
6 × 15 ml spoons olive oil
3 × 15 ml spoons red wine vinegar
1 × 5 ml spoon dried basil
1 garlic clove, crushed
1 × 5 ml spoon salt
1 × 2.5 ml spoon freshly ground black pepper

Imperial

8 oz long-grain rice
4 tablespoons dry white wine
1 green pepper, cored, seeded and thinly sliced
1 red pepper, cored, seeded and thinly sliced
1 × 4 oz can fagioli, or similar small beans, drained
1 small cucumber, peeled and diced
10 stuffed green olives, halved
2 spring onions, thinly sliced

Dressing:
6 tablespoons olive oil
3 tablespoons red wine vinegar
1 teaspoon dried basil
1 garlic clove, crushed
1 teaspoon salt
½ teaspoon freshly ground black pepper

Cook the rice in boiling salted water for 15 minutes or until tender. Drain well. Put the rice in a mixing bowl and stir in the wine. Leave to cool.
Put the green and red peppers, fagioli, cucumber, olives and spring onions in a salad bowl. When the rice is cold, add it to the vegetable mixture and stir well.
Mix together the dressing ingredients in a screw-topped jar. Add to the rice mixture and toss to coat thoroughly. Chill for 30 minutes, tossing occasionally.

Moulded cucumber and grape salad

Metric	Imperial
1 large cucumber, thinly sliced	*1 large cucumber, thinly sliced*
500 g green grapes, halved and seeded	*1 lb green grapes, halved and seeded*
425 ml water	*¾ pint water*
150 g packet lemon-flavoured jelly	*5 oz packet lemon-flavoured jelly*
3 × 15 ml spoons orange juice	*3 tablespoons orange juice*
5 × 15 ml spoons lemon juice	*5 tablespoons lemon juice*
1 × 15 ml spoon finely chopped onion	*1 tablespoon finely chopped onion*
Pinch of cayenne pepper	*Pinch of cayenne pepper*
1 × 2.5 ml spoon salt	*½ teaspoon salt*
Large pinch of freshly ground black pepper	*Large pinch of freshly ground black pepper*
Watercress to garnish	*Watercress to garnish*
Marinade:	Marinade:
3 × 15 ml spoons olive oil	*3 tablespoons olive oil*
1 × 15 ml spoon wine vinegar	*1 tablespoon wine vinegar*
Large pinch of salt	*Large pinch of salt*
Large pinch of freshly ground black pepper	*Large pinch of freshly ground black pepper*
Large pinch of dry mustard	*Large pinch of dry mustard*

Mix together the ingredients for the marinade in a medium-sized mixing bowl. Place the cucumber slices and grapes in the marinade and leave for at least 30 minutes or until you are ready to use them.

Bring 150 ml (¼ pint) of the water to the boil in a saucepan. Remove from the heat and add the jelly. Stir until dissolved, then stir in the remaining water, orange juice, lemon juice, onion, cayenne, salt and pepper. Cool the jelly until it is almost set.

With a slotted spoon, remove the grapes and cucumber slices from the marinade. Drain thoroughly.

Spoon a 1 cm (½ inch) layer of the jelly into a 1.5 litre (2½ pint) ring mould. Allow to set, then arrange the cucumber slices decoratively on the jelly. Add the grapes to the remaining jelly and pour carefully into the mould. Cover and chill for 3 to 4 hours or until completely set.

Quickly dip the mould in hot water and invert onto a serving plate. Fill the centre with watercress.

Serves 6

Egg and asparagus moulded salad

Metric	Imperial
600 ml aspic jelly	*1 pint aspic jelly*
12 asparagus spears, cooked	*12 asparagus spears, cooked*
4 hard-boiled eggs, sliced	*4 hard-boiled eggs, sliced*
Cucumber slices to garnish	*Cucumber slices to garnish*

Rinse a 1.2 litre (2 pint) plain mould in cold water. Pour in enough of the liquid aspic to make a 2.5 cm (1 inch) layer on the bottom. Place the mould in a bowl of iced water. When the aspic is almost set, arrange the asparagus spears, upright, around the sides of the mould, with their tips in the aspic.

Allow the aspic to set completely, then place a layer of eggs on top. Carefully pour some of the remaining liquid aspic over the eggs to make a 2.5 cm (1 inch) layer. (If the aspic has set by this time, melt it over a moderate heat.)

Continue making layers of egg slices and aspic until they are all used, finishing with a layer of aspic. Chill for 1½ to 2 hours, or until completely set.

To serve, dip the mould quickly into hot water and invert over a serving dish. Garnish with cucumber slices.

Serves 6

Egg and asparagus moulded salad (behind); Moulded cucumber and grape salad

SPEEDY SNACKS

Salmon dreams

Metric	Imperial
16 slices of white bread	16 slices of white bread
50 g unsalted butter	2 oz unsalted butter
1 × 215 g can red salmon, drained	1 × 7½ oz can red salmon, drained
50 g cream cheese	2 oz cream cheese
1 × 15 ml spoon grated Cheddar cheese	1 tablespoon grated Cheddar cheese
Salt	Salt
Freshly ground black pepper	Freshly ground black pepper
1 egg	1 egg
1 × 15 ml spoon milk	1 tablespoon milk
Paprika	Paprika
Fat or oil for frying	Fat or oil for frying

Cooking time: 8-10 minutes

Using a 5 to 7.5 cm (2 to 3 inch) scone cutter, cut 16 circles from the bread, and butter each circle.

Remove any skin and bone from the salmon. Mash the flesh with a fork, then stir in the cream cheese and grated cheese. Season to taste with salt and pepper. Spread the mixture thickly on half the bread circles. Top with the remaining slices and press firmly together.

Beat together the egg and milk. Season with salt, pepper and paprika. Dip the sandwiches in the beaten egg mixture and fry in shallow hot fat until crisp and golden. Drain on absorbent kitchen paper and serve hot.

Crusty chicken rolls

Metric	Imperial
50 g butter	2 oz butter
½ small onion, peeled and finely chopped	½ small onion, peeled and finely chopped
100 g cooked chicken, chopped	4 oz cooked chicken, chopped
1 × 290 g can condensed mushroom soup	1 × 10½ oz can condensed mushroom soup
1 × 15 ml spoon finely grated lemon rind	1 tablespoon finely grated lemon rind
1 × 15 ml spoon finely chopped fresh parsley	1 tablespoon finely chopped fresh parsley
Salt	Salt
Freshly ground black pepper	Freshly ground black pepper
4 long crisp rolls	4 long crisp rolls

Cooking time: 15 minutes
Oven: 200°C, 400°F, Gas Mark 6

Melt 25 g (1 oz) of the butter in a frying pan. Add the onion and fry until soft. Remove from the heat and stir in the chicken, mushroom soup, lemon rind and parsley. Add salt and pepper to taste.

Remove a slice from the top of each roll and scoop out most of the centre (use for breadcrumbs) to leave a shell. Melt the remaining butter and brush lightly inside the rolls. Divide the chicken mixture between the four rolls and place the lids on again. Arrange on a baking sheet and bake in a preheated moderately hot oven for 10 minutes. Serve at once.

Quick chicken pâté

Metric	Imperial
50 g streaky bacon, rinds removed, diced	2 oz streaky bacon, rinds removed, diced
115 g liver paste	4½ oz liver paste
100 g cooked chicken, finely chopped	4 oz cooked chicken, finely chopped
1 garlic clove, crushed	1 garlic clove, crushed
1 × 5 ml spoon finely chopped fresh parsley	1 teaspoon finely chopped fresh parsley
1 × 5 ml spoon finely chopped fresh chives	1 teaspoon finely chopped fresh chives
Large pinch of salt	Large pinch of salt
Large pinch of freshly ground black pepper	Large pinch of freshly ground black pepper

Fry the bacon, without any extra fat, for 5 minutes. Remove from the heat. Pour the fat into a mixing bowl and stir in the liver paste. Add the bacon, chicken, garlic, parsley, chives, salt and pepper and mix well.

Pack the pâté into a small earthenware dish, cover and chill for about 30 minutes before serving with hot toast.

Clockwise: Croque Monsieur (behind left); Salmon dreams;
Crusty chicken rolls; Quick chicken pâté; Potted game

Croque monsieur

Metric	Imperial
8 thin white bread slices	*8 thin white bread slices*
75 g butter	*3 oz butter*
4 slices of lean cooked ham	*4 slices of lean cooked ham*
100 g Cheddar cheese, grated	*4 oz Cheddar cheese, grated*
Fat or oil for frying	*Fat or oil for frying*

Cooking time: 10 minutes

Spread the bread with butter and cover four of the slices with the ham and cheese. Top with the remaining bread and press firmly together. Trim off the crusts. Cut each sandwich into three fingers. Fry the bread fingers in shallow hot fat until golden brown on both sides. Drain on absorbent kitchen paper and serve hot.

Potted game

Metric	Imperial
350 g cooked game (rabbit, pheasant, partridge, pigeon or mixture), finely chopped	*12 oz cooked game (rabbit, pheasant, partridge, pigeon or mixture), finely chopped*
Pinch each of dried marjoram, thyme and ground mace	*Pinch each of dried marjoram, thyme and ground mace*
Salt	*Salt*
Black pepper	*Black pepper*
75 g unsalted butter	*3 oz unsalted butter*

Cooking time: 5 minutes

Pass the game twice through the fine blade of a mincer. Season to taste with the herbs and spice, salt and pepper. Melt 50 g (2 oz) of the butter in a frying pan. Add the meat and cook for 5 minutes.
Pack the meat into 1 large or 4 small earthenware pots or jars and leave to cool.
Melt the remaining butter until foaming. Strain through muslin over the meat. Chill until the butter has set. Use in sandwich fillings or serve with hot buttered toast fingers for a filling snack.

Egg and corn savoury

Metric	Imperial
25 g butter	1 oz butter
1 garlic clove, crushed	1 garlic clove, crushed
1 medium onion, peeled and thinly sliced	1 medium onion, peeled and thinly sliced
4 slices of stale white bread, crusts removed and cut into small squares	4 slices of stale white bread, crusts removed and cut into small squares
1 × 275 g can condensed celery soup	1 × 10 oz can condensed celery soup
2 × 15 ml spoons tomato purée	2 tablespoons tomato purée
350 g frozen sweetcorn, thawed	12 oz frozen sweetcorn, thawed
1 × 425 g can celery hearts, drained	1 × 15 oz can celery hearts, drained
1 × 2.5 ml spoon salt	½ teaspoon salt
Large pinch of freshly ground black pepper	Large pinch of freshly ground black pepper
1 × 5 ml spoon paprika	1 teaspoon paprika
1 × 15 ml spoon Worcestershire sauce	1 tablespoon Worcestershire sauce
6 eggs	6 eggs
4 × 15 ml spoons milk	4 tablespoons milk
Pinch of grated nutmeg	Pinch of grated nutmeg

Cooking time: 30 minutes

Melt the butter in a saucepan. Add the garlic, onion and bread squares and cook for 5 minutes or until the onion is softened. Stir in the soup, tomato purée, corn, celery hearts, salt, pepper, paprika and Worcestershire sauce. Bring to the boil, then simmer gently for 15 minutes.

Beat the eggs, milk and nutmeg together. Stir into the pan and simmer for a further 10 minutes, or until the mixture is thick and creamy. Turn into a warmed serving dish and serve at once, with hot buttered toast.

Soufflé omelette

Metric	Imperial
2 large eggs, separated	2 large eggs, separated
2 × 15 ml spoons hot water	2 tablespoons hot water
Salt	Salt
Freshly ground black pepper	Freshly ground black pepper
15 g butter	½ oz butter

Cooking time: 5 minutes

Whisk the egg yolks with the water until pale yellow. Whisk the egg whites until stiff and fold in the yolks. Season to taste with salt and pepper.

Melt the butter in a 15 cm (6 inch) omelette pan. Pour in the egg mixture and cook gently until golden brown on the underside. Place under a preheated hot grill and cook for a few minutes or until golden brown on top. Cover with any filling used, fold in half and slide out of the pan onto a hot plate. Serve hot.

Fillings:
- 2 rashers of bacon, crisply fried and crumbled
- 2 × 15 ml spoons (2 tablespoons) finely chopped fresh herbs
- 50 g (2 oz) cooked smoked fish, flaked
- 25 g (1 oz) diced cooked ham with 25 g (1 oz) grated cheese
- 50 g (2 oz) sliced mushrooms, cooked in a little butter and lemon juice
- 1 skinned and sliced tomato, cooked with ½ peeled and sliced onion and a few chopped fresh herbs
- 4 × 15 ml spoons (4 tablespoons) soured cream mixed with a few chopped fresh chives
- 1 small green pepper, cored, seeded, sliced or chopped and cooked with 1 skinned and sliced tomato and a few chopped fresh herbs

Serves 1

Soufflé omelette; Bean rarebit; Egg and corn savoury

Bean rarebit

Metric

25 g butter
1 medium onion, peeled and finely chopped
1 garlic clove, crushed
1 green pepper, cored, seeded and thinly sliced
1 × 400 g can kidney beans, drained
1 × 425 g can baked beans
4 × 15 ml spoons tomato ketchup
1 × 15 ml spoon Worcestershire sauce
1 × 2.5 ml spoon salt
1 × 5 ml spoon freshly ground black pepper
2 × 5 ml spoons mild chilli powder
175 g Cheddar cheese, grated
4 large slices of hot buttered toast

Imperial

1 oz butter
1 medium onion, peeled and finely chopped
1 garlic clove, crushed
1 green pepper, cored, seeded and thinly sliced
1 × 14 oz can kidney beans, drained
1 × 15 oz can baked beans
4 tablespoons tomato ketchup
1 tablespoon Worcestershire sauce
½ teaspoon salt
1 teaspoon freshly ground black pepper
2 teaspoons mild chilli powder
6 oz Cheddar cheese, grated
4 large slices of hot buttered toast

Cooking time: 15 minutes

Melt the butter in a frying pan. Add the onion, garlic and green pepper and fry for 5 minutes or until the onion is soft. Stir in the kidney beans, baked beans with the can juice, ketchup, Worcestershire sauce, salt, pepper and chilli powder. Cook for a further 5 minutes, stirring from time to time.

Stir in the cheese and cook, stirring constantly, for a further 3 minutes or until the cheese has melted.

Place the hot buttered toast on four warmed serving plates and spoon the bean mixture over them. Serve at once.

Clockwise: Pipérade (top left); Eggs benedict; Yorkshire rarebit; Welsh rarebit

Pipérade

Metric

4 × 15 ml spoons olive oil
1 medium onion, peeled
and thinly sliced
2 garlic cloves, crushed
1 medium green pepper,
cored, seeded and chopped
1 medium red pepper,
cored, seeded and chopped
4 large tomatoes, skinned,
seeded and chopped
1 × 2.5 ml spoon dried
thyme
1 × 2.5 ml spoon dried
oregano
1 × 2.5 ml spoon salt
Freshly ground black
pepper
4 large eggs, lightly
beaten

Imperial

4 tablespoons olive oil
1 medium onion, peeled
and thinly sliced
2 garlic cloves, crushed
1 medium green pepper,
cored, seeded and chopped
1 medium red pepper,
cored, seeded and chopped
4 large tomatoes, skinned,
seeded and chopped
½ teaspoon dried
thyme
½ teaspoon dried
oregano
½ teaspoon salt
Freshly ground black
pepper
4 large eggs, lightly
beaten

Cooking time: 20 minutes

Heat the oil in a frying-pan. Add the onion, garlic and green and red peppers. Cook, stirring occasionally, for about 5 minutes, or until the onion is soft. Reduce the heat and add the tomatoes, thyme, oregano, salt and pepper to taste. Cook, stirring frequently, for a further 10 minutes.

Pour in the eggs and continue cooking, stirring constantly, for about 5 minutes until the eggs are cooked and set. Transfer to a warmed serving dish and serve.

58

Eggs benedict

Metric	Imperial
8 thick slices of cooked ham	8 thick slices of cooked ham
8 crumpets or muffins	8 crumpets or muffins
25 g butter	1 oz butter
8 hot poached eggs	8 hot poached eggs
Hollandaise sauce:	Hollandaise sauce:
3 egg yolks	3 egg yolks
1 × 15 ml spoon cold water	1 tablespoon cold water
125 g butter, softened	4 oz butter, softened
Large pinch of salt	Large pinch of salt
Pinch of cayenne pepper	Pinch of cayenne pepper
1 × 5 ml spoon lemon juice	1 teaspoon lemon juice
1 × 15 ml spoon single cream	1 tablespoon single cream

Cooking time: 10 minutes
Oven: 140°C, 275°F, Gas Mark 1

Place the ham slices on the grill pan and cook under a preheated grill for 2 to 3 minutes on each side. Transfer to an ovenproof dish and put in a preheated very cool oven to keep warm.

To prepare the sauce, beat the egg yolks and water together, over a pan of hot water, until the mixture is pale. Gradually beat in the butter, in small pieces, and continue beating until the mixture thickens. Add the salt, cayenne and lemon juice. Stir in the cream. Remove from the heat and keep warm.

Toast the crumpets or muffins and spread them with the butter. Arrange on warmed plates. Place a slice of ham on each crumpet or muffin and top with a poached egg. Spoon a little of the sauce over each crumpet and serve at once.

Yorkshire rarebit

Metric	Imperial
15 g butter	½ oz butter
1 × 15 ml spoon plain flour	1 tablespoon plain flour
2 × 15 ml spoons milk	2 tablespoons milk
2 × 15 ml spoons brown ale or dark beer	2 tablespoons brown ale or dark beer
1 × 2.5 ml spoon prepared French mustard	½ teaspoon prepared French mustard
Large pinch of salt	Large pinch of salt
1 × 2.5 ml spoon freshly ground black pepper	½ teaspoon freshly ground black pepper
100 g Cheddar cheese, grated	4 oz Cheddar cheese, grated
2 slices of hot buttered toast	2 slices of hot buttered toast
2 thick slices of lean cooked ham	2 thick slices of lean cooked ham
2 poached eggs, kept hot	2 poached eggs, kept hot

Cooking time: 15 minutes

Melt the butter in a saucepan. Remove from the heat and stir in the flour to make a smooth paste. Gradually stir in the milk, ale or beer, mustard, salt and pepper. Return to a low heat and cook, stirring constantly, for 2 to 3 minutes or until the mixture is thick and smooth. Add the cheese and cook, stirring constantly, for a further 2 minutes or until the cheese has melted.

Place the toast on two flameproof serving plates. Divide the cheese mixture between the toast. Place a slice of ham on each piece and place under a preheated grill. Cook for 3 to 4 minutes. Remove from the heat and place a poached egg on each piece of ham. Serve at once.
Serves 2

Welsh rarebit

Metric	Imperial
15 g butter	½ oz butter
1 × 15 ml spoon plain flour	1 tablespoon plain flour
2 × 15 ml spoons milk	2 tablespoons milk
4 × 15 ml spoons brown ale or dark beer	4 tablespoons brown ale or dark beer
2 × 5 ml spoons Worcestershire sauce	2 teaspoons Worcestershire sauce
1 × 5 ml spoon prepared English mustard	1 teaspoon prepared English mustard
1 × 2.5 ml spoon salt	½ teaspoon salt
1 × 2.5 ml spoon freshly ground black pepper	½ teaspoon freshly ground black pepper
225 g Cheddar cheese, grated	8 oz Cheddar cheese, grated
4 slices of hot buttered toast	4 slices of hot buttered toast

Cooking time: 15 minutes

Melt the butter in a saucepan. Remove from the heat and stir in the flour to make a smooth paste. Gradually stir in the milk, ale or beer, Worcestershire sauce, mustard, salt and pepper. Return to a low heat and cook, stirring constantly, for 2 to 3 minutes or until the mixture is thick and smooth. Add the cheese and cook, stirring constantly, for a further 1 minute or until the cheese has melted.

Place the toast on four flameproof serving plates. Divide the cheese mixture between the toast. Place under a preheated grill and cook for 3 to 4 minutes or until the mixture is golden brown. Serve at once.

Scampi kebabs

Metric

16 Dublin Bay prawns,
peeled
2 green peppers, cored,
seeded and cut
into 16 pieces
16 medium mushrooms
16 sage leaves
2 lemons, quartered,
then cut in half

Marinade:
4 × 15 ml spoons olive oil
2 × 15 ml spoons lemon
juice
1-2 garlic cloves,
crushed
1 × 5 ml spoon salt
1 × 2.5 ml spoon freshly
ground black pepper

Imperial

16 Dublin Bay prawns,
peeled
2 green peppers, cored,
seeded and cut
into 16 pieces
16 medium mushrooms
16 sage leaves
2 lemons, quartered,
then cut in half

Marinade:
4 tablespoons olive oil
2 tablespoons lemon
juice
1-2 garlic cloves,
crushed
1 teaspoon salt
½ teaspoon freshly
ground black pepper

Cooking time: 10 minutes

Mix together the marinade ingredients in a large, shallow mixing bowl. Add the prawns and stir well. Leave in the refrigerator to marinate for up to 1 hour.

Remove the prawns from the marinade and pat dry with absorbent kitchen paper. Reserve any remaining marinade. Thread 1 prawn onto a kebab skewer, then a piece of green pepper, a mushroom, sage leaf and lemon segment. Repeat the process 3 more times to the end of the skewer. Repeat with three more skewers. Place on the rack in the grill pan, baste with the marinade and grill for 10 minutes, turning occasionally and basting from time to time.

Remove from the heat and transfer to a warmed serving dish. Pour over the pan juices and serve with a salad.

Stuffed mushrooms

Metric	Imperial
12 large mushrooms	12 large mushrooms
1 × 5 ml spoon salt	1 teaspoon salt
1 × 2.5 ml spoon freshly ground black pepper	½ teaspoon freshly ground black pepper
1 × 5 ml spoon melted butter	1 teaspoon melted butter
25 g butter	1 oz butter
2 shallots or spring onions, peeled and finely chopped	2 shallots or spring onions, peeled and finely chopped
1 × 15 ml spoon plain flour	1 tablespoon plain flour
120 ml single cream	4 fl oz single cream
3 × 15 ml spoons finely chopped fresh parsley	3 tablespoons finely chopped fresh parsley
1.5 × 15 ml spoons grated Parmesan cheese	1½ tablespoons grated Parmesan cheese

Cooking time: 25 minutes
Oven: 190°C, 375°F, Gas Mark 5

Remove the stalks from the mushrooms and set aside. Season the mushroom caps with half of the salt and pepper and coat with the melted butter. Arrange them, hollow sides up, in a lightly greased shallow baking dish.
Finely chop the mushroom stalks. Wrap them in absorbent kitchen paper and twist to extract as much juice as possible. Melt the butter in a frying pan. Add the chopped mushroom stalks and shallots or spring onions. Fry for 3 to 4 minutes. Reduce the heat to low and stir in the flour. Cook for 1 minute. Remove from the heat and gradually stir in the cream. When the mixture is smooth, return to the heat and simmer for 2 to 3 minutes, or until thickened. Stir in the the parsley and the remaining salt and pepper.
Divide between the prepared mushroom caps. Top each with a little grated cheese. Bake in a preheated moderately hot oven for 15 minutes or until the mushrooms are tender and the stuffing is lightly browned. Serve at once.

Devilled kidneys; Stuffed mushrooms; Scampi kebabs

Devilled kidneys

Metric	Imperial
1 × 15 ml spoon oil	1 tablespoon oil
15 g butter	½ oz butter
1 medium onion, peeled and finely chopped	1 medium onion, peeled and finely chopped
100 g streaky bacon, rinds removed, finely chopped	4 oz streaky bacon, rinds removed, finely chopped
8 lamb's kidneys, cored and chopped	8 lamb's kidneys, cored and chopped
1 × 225 g can tomatoes	1 × 8 oz can tomatoes
Salt	Salt
1 × 5 ml spoon dried oregano	1 teaspoon dried oregano
1 × 2.5 ml spoon cayenne pepper	½ teaspoon cayenne pepper
1 × 15 ml spoon Worcestershire sauce	1 tablespoon Worcestershire sauce
Dash of Tabasco	Dash of Tabasco
4 × 15 ml spoons medium sherry	4 tablespoons medium sherry
1 × 15 ml spoon finely chopped fresh parsley to garnish	1 tablespoon finely chopped fresh parsley to garnish

Cooking time: 15 minutes

Heat the oil and butter together in a large frying pan. Add the onion and bacon and fry quickly until golden. Add the kidneys and brown on all sides.
Add the tomatoes with the can juice, salt to taste, oregano, cayenne, Worcestershire sauce, Tabasco and sherry. Bring to the boil, then reduce the heat and simmer, stirring occasionally, for 10 minutes. Adjust the seasoning, then serve with boiled rice, garnished with the parsley.

Open sandwiches

To live up to its Scandinavian reputation, an open sandwich should be colourful, nutritious and attractive enough to be a meal in itself. Use any combination of meat, fish, cheese, fruit, salad and vegetable in your choice. Here are a few of the more popular ones.

Ham medley

Metric	Imperial
1 slice of brown bread, buttered	*1 slice of brown bread, buttered*
2 lettuce leaves	*2 lettuce leaves*
2 slices of cooked ham, rolled	*2 slices of cooked ham, rolled*
1 × 15 ml spoon mayonnaise	*1 tablespoon mayonnaise*
Paprika	*Paprika*
2 fresh parsley sprigs	*2 fresh parsley sprigs*

Cover the slice of brown bread with the lettuce leaves. Add the rolled ham. Garnish with the mayonnaise and sprinkle with the paprika. Add the parsley sprigs.
Makes 1

Smoked salmon special

Metric	Imperial
2 slices of smoked salmon	*2 slices of smoked salmon*
1 egg, lightly scrambled	*1 egg, lightly scrambled*
1 slice of rye bread, buttered	*1 slice of rye bread, buttered*
1 small onion, peeled and sliced into rings	*1 small onion, peeled and sliced into rings*
Capers (optional)	*Capers (optional)*

Spread the salmon slices with the lightly scrambled egg and roll up. Place on top of the buttered rye bread. Garnish with onion rings and capers, if liked.
Makes 1

Harlequin delight

Metric	Imperial
1 crispbread, buttered	*1 crispbread, buttered*
50 g liver pâté	*2 oz liver pâté*
1 hard-boiled egg, sliced	*1 hard-boiled egg, sliced*
25 g cream cheese	*1 oz cream cheese*
Parsley sprigs	*Parsley sprigs*

Cover the crispbread with the liver pâté. Garnish with the hard-boiled egg, piped cream cheese and parsley sprigs.
Makes 1

Egg and bacon double-decker

Metric	Imperial
1 slice of white bread, buttered	*1 slice of white bread, buttered*
1 thin slice of soft cheese	*1 thin slice of soft cheese*
1 egg, lightly scrambled	*1 egg, lightly scrambled*
1 bacon rasher, rind removed	*1 bacon rasher, rind removed*
Parsley sprig to garnish	*Parsley sprig to garnish*

Cover the bread with the slice of soft cheese. Top with the scrambled egg. Cut the bacon rasher in half, roll up and secure with a wooden cocktail stick. Grill until crisp.
Top the scrambled egg with the rolls of bacon and garnish with the parsley sprig.
Makes 1

Top: Ham medley; Smoked salmon special. Bottom: Harlequin delight; Egg and bacon double-decker

Clockwise: Hidden cutlets (top left); Cottage cheese and grapefruit cups; Broccoli and ham rolls; Whitebait with watercress dip; Kipper kedgeree

Kipper kedgeree

Metric

100 g long-grain rice
175 g packet frozen kipper fillets
50 g butter
2 hard-boiled eggs, chopped
Salt
Freshly ground black pepper
2 × 5 ml spoons lemon juice

To garnish:
Paprika
1 hard-boiled egg, quartered

Imperial

4 oz long-grain rice
6 oz packet frozen kipper fillets
2 oz butter
2 hard-boiled eggs, chopped
Salt
Freshly ground black pepper
2 teaspoons lemon juice

To garnish:
Paprika
1 hard-boiled egg, quartered

Cooking time: 20 minutes

Cook the rice in boiling salted water for 15 minutes or until tender. Drain well.

Cook the kipper fillets according to the instructions on the packet. Remove from the bag and reserve the liquid. Skin and flake the fish.

Melt the butter in a saucepan. Add the rice, flaked fish, fish liquid and the chopped hard-boiled eggs. Heat together gently. Season to taste with salt and pepper and add the lemon juice.

Transfer to a warmed serving dish. Garnish with the paprika and quartered hard-boiled egg. Serve with toast fingers.

Hidden cutlets

Metric

175 g shortcrust pastry
(see page 74)
2 × 5 ml spoons dried
mixed herbs
Salt
Freshly ground black
pepper
4 large lamb cutlets
Beaten egg or milk to
glaze
Watercress sprigs to
garnish

Imperial

6 oz shortcrust pastry
(see page 74)
2 teaspoons dried
mixed herbs
Salt
Freshly ground black
pepper
4 large lamb cutlets
Beaten egg or milk to
glaze
Watercress sprigs to
garnish

Cooking time: 40 minutes
Oven: 200°C, 400°F, Gas Mark 6

Roll out the dough thinly on a lightly floured work surface. Brush with a little water and sprinkle with the dried herbs, then lightly with salt and pepper. Cut the dough into 2.5 cm (1 inch) strips. Carefully wrap around the cutlets, dampening the edges of the dough where necessary to make them stick, until completely enclosed.
Place on a lightly greased baking sheet and glaze with beaten egg or milk. Cook in a preheated moderately hot oven until golden brown. Garnish with the watercress and serve with a salad.

Cottage cheese and grapefruit cups

Metric

2 large grapefruit,
halved
8 lettuce leaves
350 g cottage cheese
½ small cucumber, peeled
and finely chopped

Imperial

2 large grapefruit,
halved
8 lettuce leaves
12 oz cottage cheese
½ small cucumber, peeled
and finely chopped

With a sharp knife, carefully cut around the grapefruit halves between the skin and flesh. Remove the flesh, discarding the membrane and pith, and chop into bite-sized pieces. Line each grapefruit shell with two lettuce leaves.
In a small mixing bowl, mix together the cottage cheese, diced grapefruit and chopped cucumber. Pile this mixture back into the grapefruit shells. Chill for about 30 minutes before serving.

Broccoli and ham rolls

Metric

250 g packet frozen
broccoli
4 slices of cooked ham,
at room temperature
150 ml cheese sauce, hot
(see page 71)

To garnish (optional):
Tomato wedges
Watercress sprigs

Imperial

9 oz packet frozen
broccoli
4 slices of cooked ham,
at room temperature
¼ pint cheese sauce, hot
(see page 71)

To garnish (optional):
Tomato wedges
Watercress sprigs

Cooking time: 15 minutes

Cook the broccoli in boiling water according to the directions on the packet, then drain. Place the broccoli spears on the slices of ham and roll up. Put in a flameproof dish, pour over the cheese sauce and grill under a preheated hot grill until golden brown.
Remove from the heat and garnish with the tomato wedges and watercress sprigs. Serve at once.

Whitebait with watercress dip

Metric

500 g whitebait, washed
and dried
1 egg, beaten
Plain flour
Oil for deep-frying

Dip:
½ bunch of watercress,
very finely chopped
150 ml plain unsweetened
yogurt

To garnish:
Lemon wedges

Imperial

1 lb whitebait, washed
and dried
1 egg, beaten
Plain flour
Oil for deep-frying

Dip:
½ bunch of watercress,
very finely chopped
¼ pint plain unsweetened
yogurt

To garnish:
Lemon wedges

Cooking time: 15 minutes

Coat the whitebait with the egg, then in the flour. Heat the oil to 180°C (350°F) and fry the whitebait, in batches, for 3 to 5 minutes. Drain well and keep hot. Garnish with the lemon wedges.
To make the dip, combine the watercress and yogurt. Serve separately with the whitebait.

Stir-fried bean sprouts with shredded pork

Metric

3 × 15 ml spoons oil
1 × 15 ml spoon finely
chopped onion
1 garlic clove, chopped
100 g lean pork, cut into
very thin strips
1 × 5 ml spoon salt
225 g bean sprouts
1.5 × 15 ml spoons soy
sauce
3 × 15 ml spoons chicken
stock
1 × 5 ml spoon sherry
1 × 15 ml spoon vinegar
1 × 5 ml spoon cornflour

Imperial

3 tablespoons oil
1 tablespoon finely
chopped onion
1 garlic clove, chopped
4 oz lean pork, cut into
very thin strips
1 teaspoon salt
8 oz bean sprouts
1½ tablespoons soy
sauce
3 tablespoons chicken
stock
1 teaspoon sherry
1 tablespoon vinegar
1 teaspoon cornflour

Cooking time: 5 minutes

Heat the oil in a deep-sided frying pan or wok. Add the onion, garlic, pork, salt and bean sprouts and stir-fry together for about 1½ minutes. Mix together the soy sauce, stock, sherry, vinegar and cornflour and add to the pan. Continue to stir-fry for another 1½ minutes. Serve at once.

Leeks and tomatoes à la grèque

Metric

6 medium leeks, cut into
3cm pieces
1 small onion, peeled
and sliced
6 tomatoes, skinned and
seeded
150 ml dry white wine
4 × 15 ml spoons olive oil
1 bouquet garni
½ small garlic clove
Salt
Freshly ground black
pepper

Imperial

6 medium leeks, cut into
1½ inch pieces
1 small onion, peeled
and sliced
6 tomatoes, skinned and
seeded
¼ pint dry white wine
4 tablespoons olive oil
1 bouquet garni
½ small garlic clove
Salt
Freshly ground black
pepper

Cooking time: 30 minutes

Place the leeks in a saucepan with the onion, tomatoes, wine, olive oil and enough water to cover. Add the bouquet garni and garlic and season well with salt and pepper. Bring to the boil.

Cover and simmer very gently for about 30 minutes or until the leeks are tender. Remove from the heat and allow to cool. Remove the bouquet garni and garlic before serving with crusty French bread.

Lamb chops with mint butter

Metric

4 loin or chump lamb
chops
Watercress to garnish

Marinade:
3 × 15 ml spoons oil
2 × 15 ml spoons dry
cider or white wine
½ garlic clove, crushed
Freshly ground black
pepper

Mint butter:
50-75 g butter
1 × 2.5 ml spoon vinegar
1 × 15 ml spoon finely
chopped fresh mint
Salt
Freshly ground black
pepper

Imperial

4 loin or chump lamb
chops
Watercress to garnish

Marinade:
3 tablespoons oil
2 tablespoons dry
cider or white wine
½ garlic clove, crushed
Freshly ground black
pepper

Mint butter:
2-3 oz butter
½ teaspoon vinegar
1 tablespoon finely
chopped fresh mint
Salt
Freshly ground black
pepper

Cooking time: 15 minutes

Trim the chops neatly and cut away any fat. Mix together the ingredients for the marinade with pepper to taste in a shallow dish. Place the chops in the dish and leave to marinate for 10 minutes, turning from time to time.

Remove the chops from the marinade and place on the rack of the grill pan. Cook under a preheated hot grill for about 15 minutes, turning halfway through the cooking time.

Meanwhile, prepare the mint butter. Cream the butter until soft, then gradually work in the vinegar. Beat in the mint and salt and pepper to taste. Spoon onto a square of greaseproof paper and roll up into a log shape. Chill until ready to serve.

When the chops are cooked, remove from the heat. Remove the paper from the mint butter and slice. Serve each chop topped with a slice of the mint butter and garnished with watercress. Serve with a green salad.

Clockwise: Lamb chops with mint butter; Stir-fried bean sprouts with shredded pork; Leeks and tomatoes à la grèque; Friday night special

Friday night special

Metric

1×15 *ml spoon olive oil*
1 garlic clove, finely chopped
1 onion, peeled and finely chopped
1×400 *g can tomatoes*
1×15 *ml spoon tomato purée*
1×2.5 *ml spoon caster sugar*
Large pinch of dried sage
Salt
Freshly ground black pepper
Fat or oil for frying
12 fish cakes
12 thin slices of Cheddar cheese

Imperial

1 tablespoon olive oil
1 garlic clove, finely chopped
1 onion, peeled and finely chopped
1×14 *oz can tomatoes*
1 tablespoon tomato purée
½ teaspoon caster sugar
Large pinch of dried sage
Salt
Freshly ground black pepper
Fat or oil for frying
12 fish cakes
12 thin slices of Cheddar cheese

Cooking time: 20 minutes

Heat the olive oil in a saucepan. Add the garlic and onion and cook until the onion is soft. Add the tomatoes with their juice, the tomato purée, sugar and sage. Season to taste with salt and pepper. Bring to the boil, then simmer for 5 minutes.

Heat the fat or oil in a heavy-based frying pan. Add the fish cakes and shallow fry until crisp and golden on both sides. Drain and place on the rack in the grill pan. Top each fish cake with a slice of cheese and cook under a preheated grill until the cheese melts. Arrange on a serving dish and serve the sauce separately.

Serves 4 to 6

Clockwise: Alpine fondue; Sausage skillet soufflé; Bread and cheese soup;
Oeufs de fromage en cocotte; Southern scramble

Southern scramble

Metric	Imperial
50 g unsalted butter	2 oz unsalted butter
1 small onion, peeled and finely chopped	1 small onion, peeled and finely chopped
4 large tomatoes, skinned and roughly chopped	4 large tomatoes, skinned and roughly chopped
100 g cooked ham, diced	4 oz cooked ham, diced
3 large eggs	3 large eggs
Salt	Salt
Freshly ground black pepper	Freshly ground black pepper
1 × 15 ml spoon finely chopped fresh parsley	1 tablespoon finely chopped fresh parsley

Cooking time: 10 minutes

Melt the butter in a frying pan. Add the onion and cook until it is soft. Add the tomatoes and ham and cook for 2 to 3 minutes. Lightly beat the eggs with salt and pepper to taste and stir into the pan. Continue cooking, stirring occasionally, until the eggs are just set.

Sprinkle the scrambled eggs with parsley. Serve immediately with crisp toast fingers.

Serves 2 to 4

Alpine fondue

Metric	Imperial
2 garlic cloves, halved	2 garlic cloves, halved
350 g Gruyère cheese, diced or grated	12 oz Gruyère cheese, diced or grated
150 ml milk	¼ pint milk
450 ml dry white wine	¾ pint dry white wine
1 × 15 ml spoon Kirsch	1 tablespoon Kirsch
Salt	Salt
Freshly ground white pepper	Freshly ground white pepper
1 French loaf	1 French loaf

Cooking time: 15-20 minutes

Rub the cut sides of the garlic around the sides and bottom of a cheese fondue pot. Add the cheese and milk and cook over a very low heat, stirring until the cheese melts and the mixture becomes smooth and creamy. Gradually stir in the wine and Kirsch and season with salt and pepper. Heat the fondue through without boiling.

Meanwhile, heat the French loaf in a preheated moderate oven (180°C, 350°F, Gas Mark 4) until crisp. Cut into 2.5 cm (1 inch) cubes.

Place the fondue pot over the lighted spirit burner and serve with the bread cubes.

Sausage skillet soufflé

Metric	Imperial
500 g pork sausages	1 lb pork sausages
8 tomatoes, skinned and halved	8 tomatoes, skinned and halved
3 large potatoes, peeled and cooked	3 large potatoes, peeled and cooked
50 g butter	2 oz butter
300 ml milk	½ pint milk
Salt	Salt
Freshly ground black pepper	Freshly ground black pepper
Pinch of curry powder	Pinch of curry powder
3 egg whites	3 egg whites

Cooking time: 30 minutes
Oven: 200°C, 400°F, Gas Mark 6

Fry or grill the sausages until golden brown, then cut into chunks. Place in a large casserole or ovenproof skillet. Arrange the halved tomatoes around the sausages. Mash the potatoes and butter together and stir in the milk to give a very soft consistency. Stir in salt and pepper to taste and the curry powder.

Whisk the egg whites until stiff and fold carefully into the potato mixture. Spoon around the sausages and tomatoes. Bake in a preheated moderately hot oven for about 20 minutes or until well risen and golden. Serve hot.

Oeufs de fromage en cocotte

Metric	Imperial
25 g butter or margarine	1 oz butter or margarine
4 eggs	4 eggs
1 × 2.5 ml spoon salt	½ teaspoon salt
1 × 2.5 ml spoon freshly ground black pepper	½ teaspoon freshly ground black pepper
4 × 15 ml spoons cream (optional)	4 tablespoons cream (optional)
50 g Cheddar cheese, grated	2 oz Cheddar cheese, grated

Cooking time: 15 minutes
Oven: 200°C, 400°F, Gas Mark 6

Lightly grease four individual ramekin or ovenproof dishes with the butter or margarine. Break one egg into each ramekin and sprinkle a little of the salt and pepper on each. Add a spoonful of cream to each ramekin, if using. Spread a quarter of the grated cheese over the top of each egg.

Place the ramekins in a deep roasting tin and pour enough boiling water into the tin to come halfway up the sides of the ramekins. Place in a preheated moderately hot oven and bake until the eggs are set. Serve with hot buttered toast fingers.

Bread and cheese soup

Metric	Imperial
75 g butter	3 oz butter
12 slices of French bread	12 slices of French bread
12 slices of Fontina or Gruyère cheese	12 slices of Fontina or Gruyère cheese
1.75 litres beef stock	3 pints beef stock

Cooking time: 20 minutes
Oven: 180°C, 350°F, Gas Mark 4

Melt the butter in a frying pan. Add the bread slices and fry for 3 to 4 minutes on each side or until crisp and golden. Remove from the pan and drain on absorbent kitchen paper.

Lay the bread slices on the bottom of an ovenproof soup tureen or individual ovenproof serving bowls and top with the cheese slices.

Bring the stock to the boil and pour over the bread and cheese. Cook in a preheated moderate oven for 15 minutes or until the cheese has nearly melted.

Creamy avocado pâté

Metric	Imperial
2 avocados, halved and stoned	2 avocados, halved and stoned
4 hard-boiled eggs, finely chopped	4 hard-boiled eggs, finely chopped
2 × 15 ml spoons cider or red wine vinegar	2 tablespoons cider or red wine vinegar
1 garlic clove, finely chopped	1 garlic clove, finely chopped
2 × 5 ml spoons finely chopped fresh lemon balm	2 teaspoons finely chopped fresh lemon balm
Large pinch of salt	Large pinch of salt
Pinch of freshly ground black pepper	Pinch of freshly ground black pepper
8 lettuce leaves	8 lettuce leaves
4 parsley sprigs	4 parsley sprigs

Carefully scoop out the avocado flesh, leaving the skins intact, and put the flesh in mixing bowl. Reserve the skins. Mash the avocado flesh with the eggs, vinegar, garlic lemon balm, salt and pepper to a smooth paste. Spoon the mixture back into the avocado skins.

Arrange the lettuce leaves on four individual serving plates. Top each with an avocado half. Garnish each portion with a sprig of parsley. Serve at once.

Cauliflower cheese

Metric	Imperial
1 medium cauliflower	1 medium cauliflower
Sauce:	Sauce:
25 g butter	1 oz butter
25 g plain flour	1 oz plain flour
300 ml milk	½ pint milk
Salt	Salt
Freshly ground black pepper	Freshly ground black pepper
75-100 g Gruyère or other hard cheese, grated	3-4 oz Gruyère or other hard cheese, grated

Cooking time: 15 minutes

Cook the cauliflower in boiling salted water for 8 to 10 minutes or until just tender. Drain. Arrange in a buttered flameproof serving dish and keep warm.

Meanwhile, melt the butter in a small saucepan. Stir in the flour and cook gently for 1 minute. Gradually stir in the milk. Bring to the boil and simmer, stirring, for 2 to 3 minutes or until thickened and smooth. Add salt and pepper to taste and all but 25 g (1 oz) of the cheese. Stir over a low heat to melt the cheese.

Pour the sauce over the cauliflower. Sprinkle with the remaining cheese and place under a preheated hot grill. Cook until the top is crisp and brown.

Tuna stuffed tomatoes

Metric	Imperial
1 × 200 g can tuna, drained and flaked	1 × 7 oz can tuna, drained and flaked
1 medium celery stalk, chopped	1 medium celery stalk, chopped
2 × 15 ml spoons finely chopped onion	2 tablespoons finely chopped onion
2 × 15 ml spoons finely chopped green pepper	2 tablespoons finely chopped green pepper
3 × 15 ml spoons French dressing	3 tablespoons French dressing
Salt	Salt
Freshly ground black pepper	Freshly ground black pepper
4 large tomatoes	4 large tomatoes
6 lettuce leaves	6 lettuce leaves
4 lemon slices to garnish	4 lemon slices to garnish

Mix together the tuna, celery, onion, green pepper, dressing and salt and pepper to taste. Chill.

With stem end down, cut each tomato into six wedges, cutting down to, but not through, the base. Spread the wedges apart slightly and sprinkle lightly with salt. Place the lettuce leaves on a serving plate. Put the tomatoes on the lettuce. Spoon equal amounts of the tuna mixture into the centre of each tomato. Garnish with twists of lemon and serve.

Creamy avocado pâté; Tuna stuffed tomatoes; Taramasalata; Cauliflower cheese

Taramasalata

Metric

225 g smoked cod's roe
1 small garlic clove,
finely chopped
2 small slices of white
bread, crusts removed
2 × 15 ml spoons milk
6 × 15 ml spoons oil
2 × 15 ml spoons lemon
juice
Freshly ground black
pepper

To garnish:
4 lemon slices
4 black olives

Imperial

8 oz smoked cod's roe
1 small garlic clove,
finely chopped
2 small slices of white
bread, crusts removed
2 tablespoons milk
6 tablespoons oil
2 tablespoons lemon
juice
Freshly ground black
pepper

To garnish:
4 lemon slices
4 black olives

Scoop the cod's roe out of the skin and place in a mixing bowl. Add the garlic and beat the mixture with a wooden spoon until smooth. Soak the bread in the milk for 2 to 3 minutes, then squeeze to remove as much milk as possible. Add to the cod's roe. Mix well, then add the oil, a spoonful at a time. Add the lemon juice and pepper to taste.
Divide the taramasalata between four small ramekin dishes. Garnish with a lemon slice and a black olive.

SUBSTANTIAL SNACKS

Rice balls in tomato sauce

Metric

225 g long-grain rice
1 egg, lightly beaten
1 × 15 ml spoon plain
flour
100 g Mozzarella cheese,
cubed
1 × 15 ml spoon finely
chopped fresh parsley

Sauce:
25 g butter
1 large onion (about
350 g), peeled and
finely chopped
500 g tomatoes, skinned,
seeded and chopped or
1 × 400 g can tomatoes,
drained and chopped
1 × 5 ml spoon dried basil
1 × 2.5 ml spoon dried
thyme
1 × 5 ml spoon salt
1 × 2.5 ml spoon freshly
ground black pepper
5 × 15 ml spoons dry
white wine
300 ml light stock

Imperial

8 oz long-grain rice
1 egg, lightly beaten
1 tablespoon plain
flour
4 oz Mozzarella cheese,
cubed
1 tablespoon finely
chopped fresh parsley

Sauce:
1 oz butter
1 large onion (about
12 oz), peeled and
finely chopped
1 lb tomatoes, skinned,
seeded and chopped or
1 × 14 oz can tomatoes,
drained and chopped
1 teaspoon dried basil
½ teaspoon dried
thyme
1 teaspoon salt
½ teaspoon freshly
ground black pepper
5 tablespoons dry white
wine
½ pint light stock

Cooking time: 35 minutes

The rice used in this recipe must be raw and not pre-processed. Some brands of rice are processed to ensure the grains remain separate. Such brands are not suitable for this dish.

To make the sauce, melt the butter in a saucepan. Add the onion and fry for 5 minutes or until soft. Add the tomatoes, basil, thyme, salt and pepper and cook for a further 3 minutes. Stir in the wine and stock. Bring to the boil, then simmer, covered, for 15 minutes.

Meanwhile, cook the rice in boiling salted water for 15 minutes or until tender. Drain well and allow to cool. Mix the rice with the egg and flour. Take a large spoonful of the mixture, roll into a ball and insert a cube of cheese. Completely enclose the cube of cheese. Continue making the rice balls until all the mixture and cheese have been used.

Add the rice balls to the sauce and simmer for a further 10 minutes.

To serve, turn the rice balls and the sauce into a warmed serving dish and sprinkle with the parsley.

Honey barbecued chicken

Metric

50 g butter
1 medium onion, peeled and
finely chopped
1 × 400 g can tomatoes
2 × 15 ml spoons
Worcestershire sauce
1 × 15 ml spoon clear honey
Salt
Freshly ground black
pepper
4 chicken drumsticks,
scored

To garnish:
100 g mushrooms
Parsley sprigs
Roast chestnuts
(optional)

Imperial

2 oz butter
1 medium onion, peeled and
finely chopped
1 × 14 oz can tomatoes
2 tablespoons
Worcestershire sauce
1 tablespoon clear honey
Salt
Freshly ground black
pepper
4 chicken drumsticks,
scored

To garnish:
4 oz mushrooms
Parsley sprigs
Roast chestnuts
(optional)

Cooking time: 50 minutes

Put the butter, onion, tomatoes with the can juices, Worcestershire sauce, honey and salt and pepper to taste in a saucepan. Cook gently for 30 minutes, stirring occasionally.

Place the drumsticks on the grill pan and spread liberally with the barbecue sauce. Grill the chicken under a preheated moderate grill for 10 minutes on each side, basting frequently with more of the sauce.

Halfway through the cooking, put the mushrooms on the grill pan around the chicken. Brush with the sauce and grill until cooked.

Serve the barbecued chicken on a bed of rice, garnished with the grilled mushrooms and parsley, with roast chestnuts when in season. Spoon over any remaining sauce.

Ham and fried rice; Honey barbecued chicken; Rice balls in tomato sauce

Ham and fried rice

Metric

225 g long-grain rice
15 g butter
2 eggs, lightly beaten
4 × 15 ml spoons oil
100 g French beans, cut
into small pieces,
blanched and drained
275 g cooked ham, finely
diced
1 × 2.5 ml spoon freshly
ground black pepper
4 small spring onions, cut
into 2.5 cm pieces
1 × 15 ml spoon finely
chopped fresh
coriander

Imperial

8 oz long-grain rice
½ oz butter
2 eggs, lightly beaten
4 tablespoons oil
4 oz French beans, cut
into small pieces,
blanched and drained
10 oz cooked ham, finely
diced
½ teaspoon freshly
ground black pepper
4 small spring onions, cut
into 1 inch pieces
1 tablespoon finely
chopped fresh
coriander

Cooking time: 25 minutes

Cook the rice in boiling salted water for 15 minutes or until it is tender. Drain well.

Melt the butter in a frying pan. Add the eggs and cook for 2 to 3 minutes or until they are set on the underside. Stir the eggs with a fork and cook for 2 to 3 minutes more. Transfer the eggs to a mixing bowl and break up with a fork.

Heat the oil in the frying pan. Add the cooked rice, beans, ham and pepper and cook, stirring constantly, for 2 minutes or until the rice is well coated with oil. Reduce the heat to low and add the spring onions and eggs. Cook for 2 minutes or until the mixture is hot.

Remove from the heat and transfer to a warmed serving dish. Sprinkle with the coriander and serve immediately.

73

Cream cheese and bacon quiche

Metric

175 g shortcrust pastry
dough (see below)
4 smoked streaky bacon
rashers, rinds
removed
1 egg
3 egg yolks
225 g cream cheese,
softened
150 ml double cream
Salt
Freshly ground black
pepper
3 tomatoes, skinned and
sliced

To garnish:
Bacon rolls, cooked

Imperial

6 oz shortcrust pastry
dough (see below)
4 smoked streaky bacon
rashers, rinds
removed
1 egg
3 egg yolks
8 oz cream cheese,
softened
¼ pint double cream
Salt
Freshly ground black
pepper
3 tomatoes, skinned and
sliced

To garnish:
Bacon rolls, cooked

Cooking time: 35 minutes
Oven: 200°C, 400°F, Gas Mark 6
   180°C, 350°F, Gas Mark 4

Roll out the pastry dough and use to line a 20 cm (8 inch) flan ring. Cut the bacon rashers into 5 mm (¼ inch) wide strips and fry without any fat for 3 minutes. Drain on absorbent kitchen paper, then arrange on the bottom of the flan case.

Beat the egg and egg yolks together, add the cream cheese and continue beating until the mixture is smooth. Gradually beat in the cream. Season with salt and pepper to taste and pour the mixture over the bacon. Arrange the tomatoes on top.

Bake in the centre of a preheated moderately hot oven for 20 minutes, then reduce the heat to moderate and bake for a further 10 minutes or until set. Serve the quiche garnished with bacon rolls.

Serves 4 to 6

Lample pie

Metric

225 g cooked lamb, minced
175 g cooked ham or
bacon, minced
225 g cooking apples,
peeled, cored and sliced
1 large onion, peeled
and thinly sliced
Salt
Freshly ground black
pepper
1 × 2.5 ml spoon dried
rosemary
1 × 2.5 ml spoon dried sage
300-450 ml chicken
stock
1 × 15 ml spoon tomato
purée

Pastry:
6 oz plain flour
75 g margarine
2 × 15 ml spoons water
1 egg, beaten

Imperial

8 oz cooked lamb, minced
6 oz cooked ham or
bacon, minced
8 oz cooking apples,
peeled, cored and sliced
1 large onion, peeled
and thinly sliced
Salt
Freshly ground black
pepper
½ teaspoon dried
rosemary
½ teaspoon dried sage
½-¾ pint chicken
stock
1 tablespoon tomato
purée

Pastry:
175 g plain flour
3 oz margarine
2 tablespoons water
1 egg, beaten

Cooking time: 35 minutes
Oven: 230°C, 450°F, Gas Mark 8
   180°C, 350°F, Gas Mark 4

Arrange the lamb and ham or bacon in layers with the apples and onion in a 20 cm (8 inch) buttered pie dish. Sprinkle each layer with a little salt, pepper and herbs. Mix the stock with the tomato purée and pour into the pie dish.

Sift the flour into a mixing bowl. Rub in the margarine until the mixture resembles fine breadcrumbs. Add the water and stir into a dough. Knead together on a floured worktop until smooth. Chill, then roll out into a lid to cover the pie. Place on top of the pie and seal the edges. Cut an air vent in the centre for the steam to escape. Brush the pastry with the beaten egg.

Bake in the centre of a preheated hot oven for 10 minutes, then reduce the heat to moderate and bake for a further 25 minutes. Serve hot with buttered potatoes and a green vegetable, or cold with a salad.

Serves 4 to 6

Lample pie; Cream cheese and bacon quiche; Cheese and bread bake

Cheese and bread bake

Metric

1 thick slice of white bread, cubed
200 ml milk
8 slices of white bread, crusts removed
40 g butter
3 eggs, separated
1.5 × 15 ml spoons plain flour
225 g Cheddar cheese, grated
1 × 2.5 ml spoon salt
Large pinch of grated nutmeg
100 ml single cream
1-2 bacon rashers, cooked and chopped, to garnish

Imperial

1 thick slice of white bread, cubed
⅓ pint milk
8 slices of white bread, crusts removed
1½ oz butter
3 eggs, separated
1½ tablespoons plain flour
8 oz Cheddar cheese, grated
½ teaspoon salt
Large pinch of grated nutmeg
4 fl oz single cream
1-2 bacon rashers, cooked and chopped, to garnish

Cooking time: 35-40 minutes
Oven: 180°C, 350°F, Gas Mark 4

Place the bread cubes in a shallow dish and sprinkle over half the milk. In another dish, spread out the bread slices and sprinkle with the remaining milk. Leave the bread cubes and slices to soak.

Cream the butter with the egg yolks, one at a time. Stir in the flour. Add the soaked bread cubes, cheese, salt and nutmeg. Mix well and stir in the cream.

Beat the egg whites until they are stiff. Fold into the cheese and egg mixture.

Line a greased straight-sided ovenproof dish with the soaked bread slices. Trim to fit. Pour the cheese mixture into the dish and bake in a preheated moderate oven for 35 to 40 minutes. Garnish with the bacon and serve at once.

75

Macaroni cheese

Metric	Imperial
500 g macaroni	1 lb macaroni
225 g Cheddar cheese, grated	8 oz Cheddar cheese, grated
40 g butter	1½ oz butter
40 g plain flour	1½ oz plain flour
450 ml milk	¾ pint milk
1 × 15 ml spoon Worcestershire sauce	1 tablespoon Worcestershire sauce
1 × 2.5 ml spoon salt	½ teaspoon salt
1 × 2.5 ml spoon white pepper	½ teaspoon white pepper
Pinch of cayenne pepper	Pinch of cayenne pepper

Cooking time: 35-40 minutes
Oven: 180°C, 350°F, Gas Mark 4

Cook the macaroni in boiling salted water for 10 to 12 minutes or until tender. Drain well.

Put half the macaroni in a liberally buttered casserole. Cover with half the grated cheese, then top with the remaining macaroni.

Melt the butter in a saucepan. Stir in the flour and cook for 1 minute, stirring constantly. Remove from the heat and gradually stir in the milk. Return to the heat and bring to the boil, stirring. Add the Worcestershire sauce, salt, pepper and cayenne. Simmer for 2 minutes, then pour into the casserole. Sprinkle the remaining grated cheese on top.

Bake in a preheated moderate oven for 20 to 25 minutes or until the top is golden brown. Serve immediately.

Cold curried pasta

Metric	Imperial
100 g pasta shapes	4 oz pasta shapes
½ small onion, peeled and finely chopped	½ small onion, peeled and finely chopped
2 × 15 ml spoons dry vermouth	2 tablespoons dry vermouth
5 × 15 ml spoons thick mayonnaise	5 tablespoons thick mayonnaise
1 × 5 ml spoon mild curry paste	1 teaspoon mild curry paste
1 × 5 ml spoon apricot jam	1 teaspoon apricot jam
1 × 5 ml spoon lemon juice	1 teaspoon lemon juice
2 large sausages, cooked and thinly sliced	2 large sausages, cooked and thinly sliced

To garnish:	To garnish:
1 tomato, sliced	1 tomato, sliced
Black olives	Black olives

Cooking time: 15 minutes

Cook the pasta in boiling salted water for 12 to 15 minutes or until tender. Drain well and cool.

Put the onion and vermouth in a saucepan and bring to the boil. Simmer for 3 minutes. Remove from the heat and allow to cool.

Mix together the onion mixture, mayonnaise, curry paste, apricot jam and lemon juice. Pour over the pasta and toss to coat evenly. Fold in the sausages. Turn the mixture into a serving dish and garnish with the tomato slices and black olives. Chill for 30 minutes before serving.

Serves 2

Cold curried pasta; Macaroni cheese; Vegetable pancakes; Pasta omelette

Vegetable pancakes

Metric	Imperial
4 × 15 ml spoons oil	4 tablespoons oil
2 medium onions, peeled and finely chopped	2 medium onions, peeled and finely chopped
1 small red pepper, cored, seeded and chopped	1 small red pepper, cored, seeded and chopped
½ small green cabbage, cored and shredded	½ small green cabbage, cored and shredded
1 small tart eating apple, peeled, cored and chopped	1 small tart eating apple, peeled, cored and chopped
1 × 5 ml spoon salt	1 teaspoon salt
1 × 2.5 ml spoon freshly ground black pepper	½ teaspoon freshly ground black pepper
1 × 5 ml spoon dried dill	1 teaspoon dried dill
8 × 15 cm pancakes, kept warm (see page 89)	8 × 6 inch pancakes, kept warm (see page 89)
25 g butter	1 oz butter

Cooking time: 25 minutes

Heat the oil in a frying pan. Add the onions and red pepper and fry for 5 minutes. Add the cabbage, apple, salt, pepper and dill and cook for a further 5 minutes. Remove from the heat.

Spread the pancakes out on a flat surface. Place 1 to 2 × 15 ml spoons (1 to 2 tablespoons) of the vegetable mixture on the centre of each and roll it up, completely enclosing the filling.

Arrange on a warmed shallow flameproof serving dish. Dot with the butter and grill for 5 minutes or until lightly browned. Serve hot.

Pasta omelette

Metric	Imperial
175 g wholemeal pasta shapes	6 oz wholemeal pasta shapes
6 eggs	6 eggs
1 × 15 ml spoon water	1 tablespoon water
1 × 2.5 ml spoon salt	½ teaspoon salt
1 × 2.5 ml spoon freshly ground black pepper	½ teaspoon freshly ground black pepper
50 g Mozzarella cheese, cubed	2 oz Mozzarella cheese, cubed
50 g cooked ham, diced	2 oz cooked ham, diced
4 × 15 ml spoons olive oil	4 tablespoons olive oil

Cooking time: 25 minutes

Cook the pasta in boiling salted water for 12 to 15 minutes or until tender. Drain and keep warm.

Beat together the eggs, water, salt and pepper. Stir in the cheese cubes and ham.

Heat the oil in a large omelette pan. Pour in the egg mixture. Cook for 4 minutes, lifting the set edges of the omelette to allow the liquid egg mixture to cook. Spoon the pasta onto half the omelette and gently fold the other half over. Cook for a further 2 minutes.

Remove from the heat and place under a preheated hot grill. Grill for 2 minutes or until the top is golden brown. Serve at once.

Stuffed cabbage leaves; Spicy shepherd's pie; Fricadelles

Stuffed cabbage leaves

Metric

8 large cabbage leaves
2 × 15 ml spoons olive
oil
2 onions, peeled and
finely chopped
225 g cooked chicken or
ham, minced
2 × 5 ml spoons finely
chopped fresh parsley
2 × 15 ml spoons dry
ready-prepared sage and
onion stuffing
1.5 × 5 ml spoons tomato
purée
3 × 15 ml spoons boiling
water
15 g butter
1 × 225 g can tomatoes,
drained
Salt
Freshly ground black
pepper
Pinch of ground cumin

Imperial

8 large cabbage leaves
2 tablespoons olive
oil
2 onions, peeled and
finely chopped
8 oz cooked chicken or
ham, minced
2 teaspoons finely
chopped fresh parsley
2 tablespoons dry ready-
prepared sage and onion
stuffing
1½ teaspoons tomato
purée
3 tablespoons boiling
water
½ oz butter
1 × 8 oz can tomatoes,
drained
Salt
Freshly ground black
pepper
Pinch of ground cumin

Cooking time: 40 minutes
Oven: 180°C, 350°F, Gas Mark 4

Trim the cabbage leaves into squares or rectangles and
blanch in boiling salted water for 3 minutes. Drain
thoroughly and leave to cool.

Heat the oil in a heavy-based pan. Add the onions and
fry until soft. Stir in the meat, parsley, stuffing, tomato
purée, boiling water, butter and tomatoes. Season to taste
with salt, pepper and cumin. Bring to the boil and simmer
for 5 minutes.

Spread out the cabbage leaves. Divide the filling between
them and roll the leaves into neat parcels. Place in a lightly
buttered baking dish. Cover with foil or a lid and bake in
a preheated moderate oven for 25 minutes.

Serve hot with a thick tomato sauce.

Spicy shepherd's pie

Metric	Imperial
25 g butter or margarine	1 oz butter or margarine
1 onion, peeled and finely chopped	1 onion, peeled and finely chopped
25 g plain flour	1 oz plain flour
200 ml beef stock	⅓ pint beef stock
500 g cooked lamb, minced	1 lb cooked lamb, minced
Salt	Salt
Freshly ground black pepper	Freshly ground black pepper
1 × 15 ml spoon	1 tablespoon
Worcestershire sauce	Worcestershire sauce
Pinch of grated nutmeg	Pinch of grated nutmeg
Large pinch of mild curry powder	Large pinch of mild curry powder
1 × 225 g can baked beans	1 × 8 oz can baked beans

Topping:	Topping:
500 g potatoes, peeled and cooked	1 lb potatoes, peeled and cooked
25 g butter or margarine	1 oz butter or margarine
2 × 15 ml spoons milk	2 tablespoons milk
Parsley sprig to garnish	Parsley sprig to garnish

Cooking time: 45 minutes

Melt the butter or margarine in a saucepan and fry the onion for 5 minutes. Stir in the flour and cook for 1 minute. Remove from the heat and stir in the stock, lamb, salt and pepper to taste, Worcestershire sauce, nutmeg and curry powder. Return to the heat and bring to the boil, then simmer for 30 minutes. Add the baked beans and cook for a further 3 minutes. Transfer to a flameproof dish and keep hot.

Mash the potatoes with the butter or margarine and milk. Spread the potato on top of the spicy lamb mixture and mark with a fork. Place under a preheated moderate grill and cook until golden brown. Serve at once, garnished with parsley.

Fricadelles

Metric	Imperial
500 g lean veal, minced	1 lb lean veal, minced
1 small onion, peeled and finely chopped	1 small onion, peeled and finely chopped
1 × 5 ml spoon finely chopped fresh parsley	1 teaspoon finely chopped fresh parsley
Large pinch of dried thyme	Large pinch of dried thyme
Large pinch of ground mace or grated nutmeg	Large pinch of ground mace or grated nutmeg
Salt	Salt
Freshly ground black pepper	Freshly ground black pepper
2 thin slices of white bread, crusts removed	2 thin slices of white bread, crusts removed
2 × 15 ml spoons milk	2 tablespoons milk
1 small egg, beaten	1 small egg, beaten
2 × 15 ml spoons plain flour	2 tablespoons plain flour
50 g unsalted butter	2 oz unsalted butter
300 ml tomato sauce, hot (see page 73)	½ pint tomato sauce, hot (see page 73)
Finely chopped fresh parsley to garnish	Finely chopped fresh parsley to garnish

Cooking time: 30-35 minutes
Oven: 180°C, 350°F, Gas Mark 4

Mix together the veal, onion, parsley, thyme, mace or nutmeg, and salt and black pepper to taste.

Soak the bread in the milk for a few minutes, then squeeze out the excess liquid. Mash the bread with a fork and add it to the meat mixture with the egg. Combine the mixture thoroughly using your hands. Shape into 12 fat sausages. Mix the flour with salt and pepper and use to coat the sausages.

Melt the butter in a frying pan and fry the fricadelles, in batches, until evenly brown. Transfer to a casserole. Pour over the hot tomato sauce, cover and cook in a preheated moderate oven for 15 to 20 minutes.

Serve the fricadelles hot, sprinkled with parsley, with salad or pasta.

Chicken livers with sage

Metric	Imperial
25 g butter	1 oz butter
2 bacon rashers, rinds removed, diced	2 bacon rashers, rinds removed, diced
500 g chicken livers, cut into small pieces	1 lb chicken livers, cut into small pieces
Salt	Salt
Black pepper	Black pepper
4 sage leaves, chopped	4 sage leaves, chopped
1 × 15 ml spoon sherry	1 tablespoon sherry
1 × 15 ml spoon water	1 tablespoon water
Chopped fresh parsley to garnish	Chopped fresh parsley to garnish

Cooking time: 10 minutes

Melt the butter in a small frying pan. Add the bacon and fry for 2 to 3 minutes. Add the chicken livers, salt and pepper to taste and the sage and cook for 5 minutes, stirring occasionally.

Transfer to a warmed serving dish and keep warm. Add the sherry and water to the pan and stir to mix in the sediment from the bottom. Pour these juices over the chicken liver mixture. Serve with boiled rice, garnished with parsley.

Scotch cheesies

Metric	Imperial
125 g Gorgonzola, Danish blue or Dolcelatte cheese, rind removed	4 oz Gorgonzola, Danish blue or Dolcelatte cheese, rind removed
500 g sausagemeat	1 lb sausagemeat
1 × 15 ml spoon prepared French mustard	1 tablespoon prepared French mustard
Salt	Salt
Freshly ground black pepper	Freshly ground black pepper
Plain flour	Plain flour
1 egg, beaten	1 egg, beaten
25 g dry white breadcrumbs	1 oz dry white breadcrumbs
Oil for deep frying	Oil for deep frying

Cooking time: 10 minutes

Divide the cheese into twelve even-sized pieces. Pound the sausagemeat with the mustard and salt and pepper to taste until well blended. Divide the sausagemeat into twelve portions. Roll each piece of cheese in a portion of sausagemeat, making sure the cheese is completely enclosed. Coat the balls in flour, then beaten egg, then breadcrumbs, pressing the crumbs on well. Chill for 30 minutes to set the crumbs.

Heat the oil in a deep frying pan until it is 190°C (375°F). Fry the balls until golden, then drain on absorbent kitchen paper. Serve cold with salad or pickles.

Makes 12

Turkey breasts in cider cream sauce

Metric	Imperial
2 × 15 ml spoons oil	2 tablespoons oil
2 small onions, peeled and sliced	2 small onions, peeled and sliced
2 × 225 g turkey breasts	2 × 8 oz turkey breasts
2 × 15 ml spoons plain flour	2 tablespoons plain flour
400 ml dry cider	14 fl oz dry cider
Salt	Salt
Freshly ground black pepper	Freshly ground black pepper
3 large red peppers, cored, seeded and sliced	3 large red peppers, cored, seeded and sliced
1 × 15 ml spoon cream	1 tablespoon cream

Cooking time: 20-25 minutes

Heat the oil in a frying pan. Add the onions and fry until soft but not brown. Cut the turkey breasts into eight pieces and coat in the flour. Add to the pan and fry on all sides until golden brown. Remove the turkey from the pan. Stir in any remaining flour and cook for 1 minute. Gradually add the cider, stirring constantly. Season to taste with salt and pepper and bring to the boil.

Return the turkey to the pan with the red peppers. Reduce the heat and simmer for 15 to 20 minutes, or until the turkey is cooked. Remove from the heat and stir in the cream. Serve with buttered noodles and a green salad.

Pan haggarty

Metric	Imperial
1 kg potatoes, peeled	2 lb potatoes, peeled
50 g dripping or lard	2 oz dripping or lard
500 g onions, peeled and thinly sliced	1 lb onions, peeled and thinly sliced
100 g Cheddar cheese, grated	4 oz Cheddar cheese, grated
Salt	Salt
Freshly ground black pepper	Freshly ground black pepper

Cooking time: 30-40 minutes

Cut the potatoes into 3 mm ($\frac{1}{8}$ inch) thick slices and dry on absorbent kitchen paper.

Melt the dripping or lard in a large frying pan. Arrange the potatoes, onions and cheese in layers in the pan, reserving a little cheese for the top. Begin and finish with potato slices. Season each layer with salt and black pepper. Cover the pan and cook over a low heat for 30 to 40 minutes or until the vegetables are tender. Sprinkle the remaining cheese over the top and brown under a preheated hot grill for a few minutes. Serve at once.

Chicken livers with sage; Scotch cheesies; Turkey breasts in cider cream sauce; Pan haggarty

Vegetable rissoles; Noodle savoury; Tuna cheese with dill

Vegetable rissoles

Metric	Imperial
100 g red lentils, soaked overnight, cooked and drained	*4 oz red lentils, soaked overnight, cooked and drained*
1 large onion, peeled and finely chopped	*1 large onion, peeled and finely chopped*
1 celery stalk, finely diced	*1 celery stalk, finely diced*
2 small carrots, peeled and grated	*2 small carrots, peeled and grated*
50 g French beans, cooked and finely chopped	*2 oz French beans, cooked and finely chopped*
50 g fresh white breadcrumbs	*2 oz fresh white breadcrumbs*
3 eggs	*3 eggs*
1.5 × 5 ml spoons salt	*1½ teaspoons salt*
1 × 5 ml spoon freshly ground black pepper	*1 teaspoon freshly ground black pepper*
1 × 5 ml spoon dried mixed herbs	*1 teaspoon dried mixed herbs*
75 g dry white breadcrumbs	*3 oz dry white breadcrumbs*
4 × 15 ml spoons vegetable oil	*4 tablespoons vegetable oil*

Cooking time: 15 minutes

Put the lentils, onion, celery, carrots, beans, fresh breadcrumbs, 2 of the eggs, the salt, pepper and mixed herbs in a mixing bowl. Mix well. Leave for 30 minutes.

Shape the mixture into 8 small cakes. Dip each rissole into the remaining beaten egg and then into the dry breadcrumbs.

Heat the vegetable oil in a frying pan. Add the rissoles and cook on each side for about 7 to 8 minutes or until they are golden brown. Drain on absorbent kitchen paper and serve immediately.

Tuna cheese with dill

Metric

40 g butter
1 medium onion, peeled
and finely chopped
1 × 275 g can condensed
cream of mushroom soup
Large pinch of salt
1 × 2.5 ml spoon white
pepper
1 × 5 ml spoon dried dill
1 × 275 g can tuna fish,
drained and flaked
½ × 200 g can sweetcorn,
drained
75 g Gruyère cheese,
grated
6 thin slices of Gruyère
cheese
40 g fresh breadcrumbs

Imperial

1½ oz butter
1 medium onion, peeled
and finely chopped
1 × 10 oz can condensed
cream of mushroom soup
Large pinch of salt
½ teaspoon white
pepper
1 teaspoon dried dill
1 × 10 oz can tuna fish,
drained and flaked
½ × 7 oz can sweetcorn,
drained
3 oz Gruyère cheese,
grated
6 thin slices of Gruyère
cheese
1½ oz fresh breadcrumbs

Cooking time: 20 minutes

Melt the butter in a frying pan. Add the onion and fry for 5 minutes or until soft. Stir in the soup, salt, pepper and dill and bring to the boil. Stir in the tuna fish, sweetcorn and half the grated cheese. Cook, stirring occasionally, for about 3 minutes, or until heated through.

Transfer to a flameproof serving dish. Lay the cheese slices over the top.

Mix together the remaining grated cheese and the breadcrumbs. Sprinkle this mixture over the cheese slices to cover completely. Place the dish under a preheated moderately hot grill and cook for 5 to 8 minutes or until the top is brown and bubbly. Serve at once.

Noodle savoury

Metric

6 × 15 ml spoons olive oil
2 medium onions, peeled
and thinly sliced
2 garlic cloves, crushed
1 large green pepper,
cored, seeded and sliced
175 g mushrooms, thinly
sliced
1 × 2.5 ml spoon salt
1 × 2.5 ml spoon freshly
ground black pepper
1 × 5 ml spoon dried
oregano
120 ml light stock
50 g tomato purée
750 g ribbon noodles
25 g Parmesan cheese,
grated

Imperial

6 tablespoons olive oil
2 medium onions, peeled
and thinly sliced
2 garlic cloves, crushed
1 large green pepper,
cored, seeded and sliced
6 oz mushrooms, thinly
sliced
½ teaspoon salt
½ teaspoon freshly
ground black pepper
1 teaspoon dried
oregano
4 fl oz light stock
2 oz tomato purée
1½ lb ribbon noodles
1 oz Parmesan cheese,
grated

Cooking time: 30 minutes

Heat the oil in a large saucepan. Add the onions, garlic and green pepper. Fry for 5 minutes or until the onions are soft. Add the mushrooms and cook for a further 3 minutes. Stir in the salt, pepper, oregano and stock. Bring to the boil and stir in the tomato purée. Simmer for 15 minutes.

Meanwhile, cook the noodles in boiling salted water for 10 to 12 minutes or until tender. Drain well and arrange in a warmed deep serving dish. Pour over the sauce and sprinkle with the grated Parmesan cheese.

Serves 6

Vegetable curry

Metric	Imperial
4 × 15 ml spoons oil	*4 tablespoons oil*
1 × 5 ml spoon mustard seeds, crushed	*1 teaspoon mustard seeds, crushed*
5 cm piece fresh root ginger, peeled and minced	*2 inch piece fresh root ginger, peeled and minced*
2 garlic cloves, crushed	*2 garlic cloves, crushed*
1 onion, peeled and minced	*1 onion, peeled and minced*
1 green chilli, seeded and minced	*1 green chilli, seeded and minced*
1.5 × 5 ml spoons turmeric	*1½ teaspoons turmeric*
1 × 15 ml spoon ground coriander	*1 tablespoon ground coriander*
750 g mixed vegetables (e.g. carrots, beans, aubergines, cauliflower, green peppers, potatoes, spring onions and okra), prepared and chopped	*1½ lb mixed vegetables (e.g. carrots, beans, aubergines, cauliflower, green peppers, potatoes, spring onions and okra), prepared and chopped*
1 × 5 ml spoon salt	*1 teaspoon salt*
225 g fresh coconut, puréed in a blender with 175 ml water	*8 oz fresh coconut, puréed in a blender with 6 fl oz water*
2 × 15 ml spoons chopped fresh coriander leaves (optional)	*2 tablespoons chopped fresh coriander leaves (optional)*

Cooking time: 40 minutes

Heat the oil in a large saucepan. Add the mustard seeds, ginger and garlic and fry for 30 seconds. Add the onion and green chilli and fry gently for 10 minutes, or until the onion is golden.

Stir in the turmeric and ground coriander and cook for 1 minute. Add the vegetables and stir to mix well with the fried spices. Stir in the salt and coconut purée. If the mixture is too dry add 1 to 2 × 15 ml spoons (1 to 2 tablespoons) water.

Cover the pan and simmer for 30 minutes, or until the vegetables are tender when pierced with the point of a sharp knife. Turn into a warmed serving dish, sprinkle with the chopped coriander, if used, and serve with boiled rice.

Risotto with leeks and bacon

Metric	Imperial
500 g streaky bacon rashers, rinds removed, chopped	*1 lb streaky bacon rashers, rinds removed, chopped*
4 × 15 ml spoons oil	*4 tablespoons oil*
4 leeks, chopped	*4 leeks, chopped*
500 g long-grain rice	*1 lb long-grain rice*
1 × 400 g can tomatoes	*1 × 14 oz can tomatoes*
1 × 5 ml spoon salt	*1 teaspoon salt*
1 × 5 ml spoon freshly ground black pepper	*1 teaspoon freshly ground black pepper*
1 × 2.5 ml spoon cayenne pepper	*½ teaspoon cayenne pepper*
1 × 2.5 ml spoon ground cumin	*½ teaspoon ground cumin*
1 × 5 ml spoon grated lemon rind	*1 teaspoon grated lemon rind*
900 ml chicken stock	*1½ pints chicken stock*
15 g butter	*½ oz butter*
Grated Parmesan cheese (optional)	*Grated Parmesan cheese (optional)*

Cooking time: 40-45 minutes

Fry the bacon in a saucepan for 6 to 8 minutes or until it is crisp and brown and has rendered most of its fat. Remove the bacon from the pan and set aside.

Add the oil and heat it. Add the leeks and fry for 12 minutes. Stir in the rice and fry for 5 minutes, stirring frequently. Add the tomatoes with the can juice, salt, pepper, cayenne, cumin, lemon rind and stock and bring to the boil, stirring well.

Return the bacon pieces to the pan and simmer for 15 to 20 minutes or until the rice is cooked and all the liquid has been absorbed. Serve at once, topped with a knob of butter and grated Parmesan cheese, if liked.

Vegetable curry; Risotto with leeks and bacon; Quick chicken pilaff

Quick chicken pilaff

Metric

3 chicken joints, cooked
25 g butter
4 lean bacon rashers, rinds removed, diced
1 onion, peeled and chopped
225 g long-grain rice
600 ml chicken stock, hot
Salt
Freshly ground black pepper
1 bay leaf
50 g sultanas
25 g toasted almonds, chopped
Grated Parmesan cheese

Imperial

3 chicken joints, cooked
1 oz butter
4 lean bacon rashers, rinds removed, diced
1 onion, peeled and chopped
8 oz long-grain rice
1 pint chicken stock, hot
Salt
Freshly ground black pepper
1 bay leaf
2 oz sultanas
1 oz toasted almonds, chopped
Grated Parmesan cheese

Cooking time: 35-40 minutes

Remove the meat from the chicken joints and chop into bite-sized pieces.

Melt the butter in a saucepan. Add the bacon and onion. Fry for 5 minutes or until the onion is soft. Stir in the rice, stock and salt and pepper to taste. Add the bay leaf and bring to the boil. Cover and simmer gently for about 20 minutes or until the rice is tender and the liquid has been absorbed.

Remove the lid from the pan and add the sultanas, almonds and chicken. Cook gently for a further 5 minutes, uncovered. Spoon onto a hot serving dish. Sprinkle with Parmesan cheese and serve at once.

Hamburgers with pizzaiola sauce

Egg tartlets

Metric

*175 g shortcrust pastry
dough (see page 74)
300 ml mayonnaise
1 large garlic clove,
crushed
4 × 15 ml spoons coarsely
chopped fresh basil
4 hard-boiled eggs,
finely chopped*

*To garnish:
6 slices hard-boiled egg
6 small basil or parsley
sprigs*

Imperial

*6 oz shortcrust pastry
dough (see page 74)
½ pint mayonnaise
1 large garlic clove,
crushed
4 tablespoons coarsely
chopped fresh basil
4 hard-boiled eggs,
finely chopped*

*To garnish:
6 slices hard-boiled egg
6 small basil or parsley
sprigs*

Cooking time: 15 minutes
Oven: 200°C, 400°F, Gas Mark 6

Roll out the dough to 5 mm (¼ inch) thick. Using a 10 cm (4 inch) cutter, cut the dough into six circles. Line six 7.5 cm (3 inch) fluted tartlet tins with the dough, trimming off any excess. Place on a baking sheet and bake blind in a preheated moderately hot oven for 15 minutes. Remove from the tins and allow to cool.

Mix the mayonnaise, garlic and basil together. Divide the chopped egg between the pastry cases and pour over enough of the mayonnaise mixture to fill the cases.

Garnish each tartlet with a slice of hard-boiled egg and a sprig of basil or parsley. Serve cold.
Makes 6 tartlets

Cornish pasties

Metric

*225 g shortcrust pastry,
made with 225 g plain
flour, 125 g margarine
and 2-3 × 15 ml spoons
water (see page 74)
175 g stewing beef, cooked
and very thinly sliced
2 potatoes, peeled and
coarsley grated
1 onion, peeled and
finely chopped
Salt
Black pepper
15 g unsalted butter
1 egg, beaten*

Imperial

*8 oz shortcrust pastry,
made with 8 oz plain
flour, 4 oz margarine
and 2-3 tablespoons
water (see page 74)
6 oz stewing beef, cooked
and very thinly sliced
2 potatoes, peeled and
coarsley grated
1 onion, peeled and
finely chopped
Salt
Black pepper
½ oz unsalted butter
1 egg, beaten*

Cooking time: 40 minutes
Oven: 220°C, 425°F, Gas Mark 7
　　　180°C, 350°F, Gas Mark 4

Roll out the dough to about 5 mm (¼ inch) thick. Using a saucer as a guide, cut out four circles.

Mix the meat with the vegetables and salt and pepper to taste. Divide this filling between the dough circles. Top each with a piece of butter. Dampen the pastry edges with cold water and carefully draw up two edges to meet on top of the filling. Pinch and twist the pastry firmly together to a neat fluted curved pattern. Cut a small air vent in the side of each pasty.

Brush with the egg and place on a greased baking sheet. Bake in the centre of a preheated hot oven for 10 minutes. Reduce the temperature to moderate and bake for a further 30 minutes. Serve hot with a salad, or cold.

Hamburgers with pizzaiola sauce

Metric

500 g minced beef
1 onion, peeled and finely
grated (optional)
1 egg, lightly beaten
Salt
Black pepper
2 × 5 ml spoons
Worcestershire sauce

Sauce:
2 × 5 ml spoons oil
2 medium onions, peeled
and minced
2 garlic cloves, minced
2 small green peppers,
cored, seeded and sliced
crossways into rings
50 g mushrooms, chopped
1 × 400 g can tomatoes
2 × 5 ml spoons dried
marjoram or oregano
Dash of hot chilli sauce

Imperial

1 lb minced beef
1 onion, peeled and finely
grated (optional)
1 egg, lightly beaten
Salt
Black pepper
2 teaspoons
Worcestershire sauce

Sauce:
2 teaspoons oil
2 medium onions, peeled
and minced
2 garlic cloves, minced
2 small green peppers,
cored, seeded and sliced
crossways into rings
2 oz mushrooms, chopped
1 × 14 oz can tomatoes
2 teaspoons dried
marjoram or oregano
Dash of hot chilli sauce

Cooking time: 30 minutes

Mix the beef with the onion, if used. Mix in the egg, salt and pepper to taste and the Worcestershire sauce. Divide into four equal pieces and shape into hamburgers about 2 cm (¾ inch) thick.

Heat the oil in a frying pan. Add the onions and garlic and fry until they are golden. Add the pepper rings and continue cooking for 15 minutes.

Stir in the mushrooms, tomatoes with the can juice and the marjoram or oregano. Season to taste with the chilli sauce, salt and pepper. Cover and continue cooking for a further 10 minutes.

Meanwhile place the hamburgers on a grill pan. Cook under a preheated hot grill until rare or medium, to your taste. Arrange the hamburgers on a hot serving dish and pour the sauce over them. Serve with a crisp green salad.

Egg tartlets; Cornish pasties

Tomato and anchovy stuffed cod steaks

Metric

4 × 15 ml spoons olive oil
1 small onion, peeled and
thinly sliced
1 garlic clove, chopped
1 green pepper, cored,
seeded and thinly sliced
1 × 50 g can anchovy
fillets, drained and
chopped
50 g black olives, stoned
Large pinch of fennel seed
8 × 100 g cod steaks
3 small tomatoes, thinly
sliced
1 × 2.5 ml spoon salt
Large pinch of freshly
ground black pepper
1 × 65 g can tomato purée
120 ml dry red wine

Imperial

4 tablespoons olive oil
1 small onion, peeled and
thinly sliced
1 garlic clove, chopped
1 green pepper, cored,
seeded and thinly sliced
1 × 2 oz can anchovy
fillets, drained and
chopped
2 oz black olives, stoned
Large pinch of fennel seed
8 × 4 oz cod steaks
3 small tomatoes, thinly
sliced
½ teaspoon salt
Large pinch of freshly
ground black pepper
1 × 2½ oz can tomato purée
4 fl oz dry red wine

Cooking time: 35-40 minutes
Oven: 200°C, 400°F, Gas Mark 6

Heat 2 × 15 ml spoons (2 tablespoons) of the oil in a frying pan. Add the onion, garlic and green pepper. Fry for 5 minutes or until the onion is soft. Remove from the heat and stir in the anchovies, olives and fennel seed.

Place four of the cod steaks in a greased ovenproof dish and spread the anchovy mixture over them. Top each cod steak with another cod steak. Arrange the sliced tomatoes on top. Brush with the remaining oil and sprinkle with the salt and pepper.

Mix together the tomato purée and wine and pour over the fish. Bake in a preheated moderately hot oven for 30 minutes, basting from time to time. Serve at once.

Smoked haddock pancakes

Metric

Pancake batter:
125 g plain flour
Pinch of salt
1 egg
1 egg yolk
300 ml milk
1 × 15 ml spoon melted
butter or oil

Filling:
100 g unsalted butter
1 small onion, peeled and
finely chopped
2 × 15 ml spoons finely
chopped celery
100 g mushrooms, chopped
1 × 400 g can tomatoes
Pinch of caster sugar
Salt
Freshly ground black
pepper
225 g smoked haddock,
fillet, cooked, skinned and
flaked
Lemon juice
4 × 15 ml spoons grated
Cheddar cheese

To garnish:
Lemon wedges
Parsley sprigs

Imperial

Pancake batter:
4 oz plain flour
Pinch of salt
1 egg
1 egg yolk
½ pint milk
1 tablespoon melted
butter or oil

Filling:
4 oz unsalted butter
1 small onion, peeled and
finely chopped
2 tablespoons finely
chopped celery
4 oz mushrooms, chopped
1 × 14 oz can tomatoes
Pinch of caster sugar
Salt
Freshly ground black
pepper
8 oz smoked haddock
fillet, cooked, skinned and
flaked
Lemon juice
4 tablespoons grated
Cheddar cheese

To garnish:
Lemon wedges
Parsley sprigs

Cooking time: 30 minutes

Sift the flour and salt into a mixing bowl and hollow out the centre. Add the egg, egg yolk and half the milk. Stir the liquid ingredients and gradually draw in the flour. Beat well to form a smooth batter. Beat in the remaining milk and, just before using, stir in the melted butter or oil. Heat a 15 cm (6 inch) frying pan and brush lightly with oil. Pour in just enough batter to cover the surface lightly. Cook over a high to moderate heat until lightly browned. Turn and cook for 1 more minute. Make eight pancakes in this way. Keep warm.

Melt 40 g (1½ oz) of the butter in a frying pan. Add the onion, celery and mushrooms and fry until soft. Add the tomatoes with the can juice, and season with sugar, salt and pepper. Bring to the boil and simmer until the mixture is reduced to a thick purée. Remove from the heat and fold in the haddock. Sharpen to taste with lemon juice.

Spread the pancakes flat. Spoon 2 × 15 ml spoons (2 table-spoons) of the filling down the centre of each pancake and fold the sides over to make an envelope. Arrange the stuffed pancakes side by side in a shallow flameproof dish.

Melt the remaining butter and pour it over the pancakes. Sprinkle with the grated cheese and cook under a preheated hot grill until the cheese is bubbly and golden.

Garnish the pancakes with lemon wedges and sprigs of parsley. Serve at once.

Tomato and anchovy stuffed cod steaks; Smoked haddock pancakes; Fisherman's pie

Fisherman's pie

Metric

75 g butter
40 g plain flour
600 ml milk
225 g white fish fillets,
cooked, skinned and flaked
225 g smoked haddock,
cooked, skinned and flaked
4 × 15 ml spoons lemon
juice
2 × 15 ml spoons finely
chopped fresh parsley
½ small green pepper,
cored, seeded and chopped
2 hard-boiled eggs,
chopped
Salt
Freshly ground black
pepper
175 g self-raising flour
2 × 5 ml spoons prepared
mustard
75 g Cheddar cheese,
grated

Imperial

3 oz butter
1½ oz plain flour
1 pint milk
8 oz white fish fillets,
cooked, skinned and flaked
8 oz smoked haddock,
cooked, skinned and flaked
4 tablespoons lemon
juice
2 tablespoons finely
chopped fresh parsley
½ small green pepper,
cored, seeded and chopped
2 hard-boiled eggs,
chopped
Salt
Freshly ground black
pepper
6 oz self-raising flour
2 teaspoons prepared
mustard
3 oz Cheddar cheese,
grated

Cooking time: 25-30 minutes
Oven: 220°C, 425°F, Gas Mark 7

Melt 40 g (1½ oz) of the butter in a saucepan. Add the plain flour and cook, stirring, for 1 minute. Gradually stir in 450 ml (¾ pint) of the milk and bring to the boil, stirring constantly. Simmer for 2 minutes. Stir in the fish, lemon juice, parsley, green pepper, eggs and salt and pepper to taste. Spoon into a round 1 litre (2 pint) ovenproof dish.
Sift the self-raising flour into a bowl and rub in the remaining butter. Add the mustard and cheese and enough of the remaining milk to make a soft pliable dough. Knead this on a floured surface and roll out to the size of the dish. Cut the pastry into eight triangles and place over the fish so that the points meet in the centre. Brush with milk and bake in the centre of a preheated hot oven for 25 minutes or until golden.

Stuffed and baked potatoes

Baked potatoes are doubly delicious when the flesh is scooped out, mixed with other savoury ingredients, returned to the skin and baked until crisp and golden. First bake the potatoes in their jackets. Remove from the oven and slice the top from the flat side of the potato. Scoop out the potato to within 5 mm ($\frac{1}{4}$ inch) of the skin. Mix the flesh with the other filling in-gredients and return to the potato skins. Place in a roasting tin and bake in a preheated moderately hot oven until the filling is golden brown.

Cooking time: 10 minutes
Oven: 190°C, 375°F, Gas Mark 5

Spicy sausage filling

Metric

Flesh from 4 potatoes, baked in their jackets
50 g butter, softened
1 × 15 ml spoon finely chopped fresh chives
1 × 15 ml spoon American mustard
Salt
Freshly ground black pepper
4 pork sausages, cooked and sliced
50 g cheese, grated

Imperial

Flesh from 4 potatoes, baked in their jackets
2 oz butter, softened
1 tablespoon finely chopped fresh chives
1 tablespoon American mustard
Salt
Freshly ground black pepper
4 pork sausages, cooked and sliced
2 oz cheese, grated

Mix together the potato flesh, butter, chives, mustard, salt and pepper to taste, most of the sausages and the grated cheese. Combine thoroughly. Return the mixture to the potato skins and garnish with the remaining sausage slices. Bake.

Shrimp and spring onion filling

Metric

Flesh from 4 potatoes, baked in their jackets
100 g peeled shrimps
4 spring onions, finely chopped
1 × 2.5 ml spoon finely grated lemon rind
1 × 2.5 ml spoon finely chopped fresh parsley
Large pinch of cayenne pepper
50 g butter, softened
Unpeeled shrimps, to garnish

Imperial

Flesh from 4 potatoes, baked in their jackets
4 oz peeled shrimps
4 spring onions, finely chopped
½ teaspoon finely grated lemon rind
½ teaspoon finely chopped fresh parsley
Large pinch of cayenne pepper
2 oz butter, softened
Unpeeled shrimps, to garnish

Mix together the potato flesh, shrimps, spring onions, lemon rind, parsley, cayenne and butter. Beat until thoroughly mixed. Return to the potato skins and bake. Serve garnished with unpeeled shrimps.

Clockwise: Chive and cheese filling (top); Spicy sausage filling; Bacon and mushroom filling; Shrimp and spring onion filling

Chive and cheese filling

Metric

Flesh from 4 potatoes,
baked in their jackets
50 g Brie cheese, rinded
1 × 2.5 ml spoon dried
chives
1 × 2.5 ml spoon salt
1 egg yolk
50 g butter, softened
Chopped fresh chives
to garnish

Imperial

Flesh from 4 potatoes,
baked in their jackets
2 oz Brie cheese, rinded
½ teaspoon dried
chives
½ teaspoon salt
1 egg yolk
2 oz butter, softened
Chopped fresh chives
to garnish

Mix together the potato flesh, Brie, dried chives, salt, egg yolk and butter. Beat with a wooden spoon until thoroughly mixed. Return to the potato skins and bake. Serve garnished with the fresh chives.

Bacon and mushroom filling

Metric

Flesh from 4 potatoes,
baked in their jackets
4 bacon rashers, grilled
until crisp and crumbled
25 g butter
100 g mushrooms, chopped
1 × 2.5 ml spoon salt
Black pepper
Bacon rolls to garnish

Imperial

Flesh from 4 potatoes,
baked in their jackets
4 bacon rashers, grilled
until crisp and crumbled
1 oz butter
4 oz mushrooms, chopped
½ teaspoon salt
Black pepper
Bacon rolls to garnish

Mix together the potato flesh and bacon. Melt the butter in a frying pan. Add the mushrooms and fry for 3 minutes. Remove from heat and stir the mushrooms into the bacon and potato mixture with the salt and pepper. Return to the potato skins and bake. Serve garnished with crisply grilled bacon rolls.

Eggs flamenco

Metric	Imperial
4 × 15 ml spoons olive oil	4 tablespoons olive oil
1 medium onion, peeled and thinly sliced	1 medium onion, peeled and thinly sliced
2 garlic cloves, crushed	2 garlic cloves, crushed
225 g lean bacon, rinds removed, diced	8 oz lean bacon, rinds removed, diced
2 small red peppers, cored, seeded and sliced	2 small red peppers, cored, seeded and sliced
6 medium tomatoes, skinned and thinly sliced	6 medium tomatoes, skinned and thinly sliced
100 g mushrooms, thinly sliced	4 oz mushrooms, thinly sliced
1 × 2.5 ml spoon salt	½ teaspoon salt
Large pinch of freshly ground black pepper	Large pinch of freshly ground black pepper
Pinch of cayenne pepper	Pinch of cayenne pepper
1 × 15 ml spoon finely chopped fresh parsley	1 tablespoon finely chopped fresh parsley
1 × 225 g can sweetcorn, drained	1 × 8 oz can sweetcorn, drained
4 large eggs	4 large eggs

Cooking time: 45-50 minutes
Oven: 180°C, 350°F, Gas Mark 4

Heat the oil in a frying pan. Add the onion and garlic and cook for 5 minutes, or until the onion is soft. Add the bacon and red peppers and fry for 10 to 12 minutes or until the peppers are soft. Stir in the tomatoes, mushrooms, salt, pepper, cayenne and parsley and continue cooking for 5 more minutes, or until the tomatoes begin to pulp. Stir in the sweetcorn and remove from the heat.

Pour the mixture into a heavy-based ovenproof serving dish. Using the back of a spoon, make four small depressions in the vegetable mixture. Break an egg into each depression. Place the dish in the centre of a preheated moderate oven and bake for 15 to 20 minutes or until the eggs have set. Serve hot.

Corn soufflé

Metric	Imperial
2 × 15 ml spoons dry breadcrumbs	2 tablespoons dry breadcrumbs
600 ml milk	1 pint milk
1 bay leaf	1 bay leaf
1 blade of mace	1 blade of mace
1 slice of onion	1 slice of onion
6 black peppercorns, slightly crushed	6 black peppercorns, slightly crushed
1 × 5 ml spoon salt	1 teaspoon salt
25 g butter	1 oz butter
2 × 15 ml spoons plain flour	2 tablespoons plain flour
1 × 275 g can sweetcorn, drained	1 × 10 oz can sweetcorn, drained
Large pinch of white pepper	Large pinch of white pepper
3 egg yolks	3 egg yolks
75 g Cheddar cheese, grated	3 oz Cheddar cheese, grated
4 egg whites	4 egg whites

Cooking time: 30 minutes
Oven: 190°C, 375°F, Gas Mark 5

Coat the bottom and sides of a greased 1.2 litre (2 pint) soufflé dish with the breadcrumbs, pressing them on with your fingertips.

Heat the milk gently in a saucepan with the bay leaf, mace, onion slice, peppercorns and 1 × 2.5 ml spoon (½ teaspoon) of the salt for about 7 minutes, so that the milk becomes infused with the flavourings. Remove from the heat and strain the milk.

Melt the butter in the cleaned-out saucepan. Add the flour and stir to make a smooth paste. Gradually add the milk, stirring constantly. Bring to the boil, stirring. Simmer for 2 to 3 minutes or until thick and smooth. Remove from the heat and stir in the sweetcorn, remaining salt and the pepper. Allow to cool slightly.

Add the egg yolks, one at a time, beating well between each addition. Gradually stir in the cheese. Beat the egg whites until stiff and fold into the corn mixture.

Spoon into the prepared soufflé dish. Bake in a preheated moderately hot oven for 25 to 30 minutes or until the soufflé is puffed up and lightly golden. Serve at once.

Eggs flamenco; Corn soufflé; Barbecued spare ribs

Barbecued spare ribs

Metric

12-16 pork spare ribs
2 × 15 ml spoons clear
honey
3 × 15 ml spoons soy sauce
3 × 15 ml spoons tomato
ketchup
Tabasco sauce
1 small garlic clove,
crushed
Dry mustard
Paprika
Salt
Freshly ground black
pepper
4 × 15 ml spoons orange
juice
4 × 15 ml spoons wine
vinegar

Imperial

12-16 pork spare ribs
2 tablespoons clear
honey
3 tablespoons soy sauce
3 tablespoons tomato
ketchup
Tabasco sauce
1 small garlic clove,
crushed
Dry mustard
Paprika
Salt
Freshly ground black
pepper
4 tablespoons orange
juice
4 tablespoons wine
vinegar

Cooking time: 45 minutes
Oven: 180°C, 350°F, Gas Mark 4

If not already done, separate the meat into individual ribs.
Cook under a preheated moderate grill for 15 minutes or
until brown, turning several times. Arrange in a single layer
in a roasting tin.

Mix together the honey, soy sauce, tomato ketchup, a few
drops of Tabasco, the garlic and mustard, paprika, salt and
pepper to taste. Stir in the orange juice and vinegar. Pour
over the spare ribs.

Cook, uncovered, in a preheated moderate oven for 30
minutes. Serve piping hot in the sauce.

93

Ratatouille

Metric	Imperial	Cooking time: 50-55 minutes

Metric	Imperial
25 g butter	1 oz butter
4 × 15 ml spoons olive oil	4 tablespoons olive oil
2 large onions, peeled and thinly sliced	2 large onions, peeled and thinly sliced
2 garlic cloves, crushed	2 garlic cloves, crushed
2 medium aubergines, chopped	2 medium aubergines, chopped
1 large green pepper, cored, seeded and chopped	1 large green pepper, cored, seeded and chopped
1 large red pepper, cored, seeded and chopped	1 large red pepper, cored, seeded and chopped
500 g courgettes, sliced	1 lb courgettes, sliced
1 × 400 g can tomatoes	1 × 14 oz can tomatoes
1 × 5 ml spoon dried basil	1 teaspoon dried basil
1 × 5 ml spoon dried rosemary	1 teaspoon dried rosemary
1.5 × 5 ml spoons salt	1½ teaspoons salt
1 × 5 ml spoon freshly ground black pepper	1 teaspoon freshly ground black pepper
2 × 15 ml spoons finely chopped fresh parsley	2 tablespoons finely chopped fresh parsley

Melt the butter with the oil in a saucepan. Add the onions and garlic and fry for 5 minutes or until soft.

Add the aubergines, green and red peppers and courgettes. Cook for 5 minutes, stirring occasionally. Stir in the tomatoes with the juice, the basil, rosemary, salt and pepper. Sprinkle over the parsley.

Bring to the boil, then cover and simmer for 40 to 45 minutes or until the vegetables are tender but still quite firm. Remove from heat and serve at once. Or allow to cool and serve cold.

Serves 4 to 6

Jiffy pizza

Metric	Imperial	Cooking time: 25-30 minutes
		Oven: 220°C, 425°F, Gas Mark 7

Metric	Imperial
225 g self-raising flour	8 oz self-raising flour
1 × 5 ml spoon baking powder	1 teaspoon baking powder
1 × 2.5 ml spoon salt	½ teaspoon salt
25 g butter	1 oz butter
50 g Cheddar cheese, grated	2 oz Cheddar cheese, grated
150 ml milk	¼ pint milk

Topping:	Topping:
2 × 15 ml spoons oil	2 tablespoons oil
1 medium onion, peeled and finely chopped	1 medium onion, peeled and finely chopped
2 × 15 ml spoons tomato purée	2 tablespoons tomato purée
Pinch of dried oregano	Pinch of dried oregano
Pinch of dried marjoram	Pinch of dried marjoram
Salt	Salt
Freshly ground black pepper	Freshly ground black pepper
50 g Cheddar cheese, grated	2 oz Cheddar cheese, grated
1 × 50 g can anchovy fillets, drained	1 × 2 oz can anchovy fillets, drained
Few black olives	Few black olives

Sift the flour, baking powder and salt into a mixing bowl. Rub in the butter and add the grated cheese. Stir in the milk and mix to a rough dough. Turn onto a floured surface and knead lightly until smooth. Leave to rest while you prepare the filling.

Heat the oil in a small saucepan. Add the onion and fry for 5 minutes or until soft. Stir in the tomato purée, herbs and salt and pepper to taste. Cook for a further 2 minutes, then remove from the heat.

Roll out the prepared dough to a circle about 23 cm (9 inches) in diameter. Slide onto a greased baking sheet. Spread the tomato mixture over the surface right to the edges. Sprinkle with the grated cheese and top with a lattice of anchovy fillets and olives. Bake in the centre of a preheated hot oven for 20 to 25 minutes or until well risen and golden. Cut into wedges and serve warm.

Serves 4 to 6

Ratatouille; Chicken and ham loaf; Jiffy pizza

Chicken and ham loaf

Metric

1 crusty sandwich loaf
75 g butter
2 small onions, peeled and finely chopped
225 g mushrooms, thinly sliced
1 × 15 ml spoon finely chopped fresh parsley
Salt
Freshly ground black pepper
225 g sausagemeat
175 g lean bacon, diced
225 g cooked ham, diced
2 × 15 ml spoons dry sherry (optional)
Large pinch of dried sage
Large pinch of dried thyme
225 g cooked chicken, diced

Imperial

1 crusty sandwich loaf
3 oz butter
2 small onions, peeled and finely chopped
8 oz mushrooms, thinly sliced
1 tablespoon finely chopped fresh parsley
Salt
Freshly ground black pepper
8 oz sausagemeat
6 oz lean bacon, diced
8 oz cooked ham, diced
2 tablespoons dry sherry (optional)
Large pinch of dried sage
Large pinch of dried thyme
8 oz cooked chicken, diced

Cooking time: 1¼ hours
Oven: 190°C, 375°F, Gas Mark 5

Cut a 1 cm (½ inch) lengthways slice off the top of the loaf and carefully pull out the soft bread inside. Leave 1 cm (½ inch) inner lining of bread to keep the shape. Reserve the bread from inside the loaf.

Melt 50 g (2 oz) of the butter and brush most of this on the loaf, inside and out. Replace the lid and brush with the remaining melted butter. Put the loaf on a baking sheet in the centre of a preheated moderately hot oven. Bake for 10 minutes or until crisp and golden. Leave to cool.

Melt the remaining butter in a frying pan. Add the onions and fry for 5 minutes or until soft. Add the mushrooms and cook for a further 2 minutes. Stir in the parsley and season to taste with salt and pepper. Remove from the heat. Mix together the sausagemeat, bacon, ham and 3 × 15 ml spoons (3 tablespoons) of breadcrumbs made from the removed bread. Stir in the sherry and herbs and season to taste with salt and pepper. Press half the sausage mixture into the loaf case. Cover with half the onion and mushroom mixture. Arrange the chicken on top and cover with the remaining onion and mushroom and sausagemeat mixtures. Replace the lid and wrap the loaf in foil. Return to the centre of the oven and bake for 1 hour.

Serve the loaf hot or cold, cut into thick slices.
Serves 6 to 8

Index